'What we believe has a huge impact on the way we live. Our theology determines our strategy. That's what makes this book such great value. Not only does it provide an extraordinarily accessible and succinct overview of the challenge presented by Tom Wright's ground-breaking work around the life and message of Jesus and the early church – it's also a thought-provoking account of its practical outworking through a local church and in a local community.'

Steve Chalke MBE
Founder of Oasis Global and Leader of Church.co.uk, London
UN Special Advisor on Community Action Against Human Trafficking

'In this book Stephen Kuhrt offers us two very important things: not only has he pulled together the many different strands of Tom Wright's thinking into a thoughtful and readable whole, he also makes available to us the quite considerable reflections of someone who has, over the years, sought to put this theology into practice in his own ministry. *Tom Wright For Everyone* is thought-provoking, reflective, challenging and well worth reading.'

Paula Gooder, Writer and Lecturer in New Testament Studies

'Stephen Kuhrt's book makes a warm and convincing case that Tom Wright's theology has the potential to transform the local church, the academy and contemporary evangelicalism. This is a timely and accessible introduction to the significance of a formidable thinker and brave servant of God.'

John Pritchard, Bishop of Oxford

'The best theology has to be able to go beyond the academy into the everyday life of Christians. It has to be transformative for what we think and what we do. Stephen Kuhrt shows in this excellent book that Tom Wright's theology is all of that. And through his insights and practical wisdom Stephen offers his own challenge to the church today.'

Elaine Storkey, Director of Education and
Training Church Army, President of Tearfund

'Making good theology accessible and demonstrating its relevance for Christian life is an urgent need today. Stephen Kuhrt's book will be a very valuable contribution in narrowing the gap between the academy and the church, a gap which has often yawned far too wide.'

Graham Tomlin, Dean, St Mellitus College

Stephen Kuhrt became curate of Christ Church, New Malden in 2003 and its vicar in 2007. Before training for ordination he taught History and Religious Studies at Archbishop Tenison's School in Croydon. He trained for ordination at Wycliffe Hall where he gained a First in Theology at Oxford University. He is a member of the leadership team of Fulcrum, a group seeking to renew the evangelical centre of the Church of England. He has previously published *Church Growth Through the Full Welcome of Children: The Sssh Free Church* (Grove, 2009).

TOM WRIGHT FOR EVERYONE

Putting the theology of N. T. Wright into practice in the local church

Stephen Kuhrt

For Katie

and in memory of Philip King
(1935–2006)
May he rest in peace and rise in glory

First published in Great Britain in 2011

Society for Promoting Christian Knowledge
36 Causton Street
London SW1P 4ST
www.spckpublishing.co.uk

Copyright © Stephen Kuhrt 2011

British Library Cataloguing-in-Publication Data
A catalogue record for this book is available from the British Library

ISBN 978–0–281–06393–2

1 3 5 7 9 10 8 6 4 2

Typeset by Graphicraft Ltd, Hong Kong
Printed in Great Britain by Ashford Colour Press

Produced on paper from sustainable forests

Contents

Preface

It is sometimes said that the sign of someone called to be a teacher is when they possess the desire to pass on the things from which they have benefited. Having been a schoolteacher for seven years and a clergyman for a further seven, I know very well that extra motivation that comes with the opportunity to share those thoughts, ideas and experiences that I have found inspiring. Often the process towards such a goal is difficult, causing the teacher to use every tool they can find to achieve this objective. These can include simplifying and 'breaking down' the material and using stories and illustrations, frequently drawn from one's own personal experience. Throughout this process, the vision continuing to motivate 'the teacher' and the search for whatever model of learning will work is their earnest desire to pass on to others something that they have found to be immensely valuable and life-changing.

In the case of this book, that 'something' is the theology and biblical scholarship of Tom Wright. I know that I am just one of many Christians, particularly in the UK and the USA, for whom over the last ten or so years the encounter with Tom Wright's work has been truly life-changing. In my particular case, it is engagement with Wright's work, more than that of any other writer, which has transformed the way in which I now read the New Testament and therefore understand my own personal Christian life and vocation. Beyond this and very much flowing from it, Wright's theology has then gone on to have immense influence upon how I seek to lead the worship and mission of the church of which I am Vicar, Christ Church, New Malden in Surrey, England.[1]

However, for all the Christians I encounter who speak in very similar terms of the influence of Wright's work, I meet a much greater number for whom his theology remains, at least partially, a closed book. The reasons for this, I believe, are various and in the following chapters a number of suggestions for why this is the case will be made, including some that are controversial. But in the first instance this book has been written with the positive aim of helping to make Tom Wright's theology more accessible to those growing number of clergy, ordinands and lay people deeply attracted to what they have grasped about his thought and who are keen to understand more. Reflecting what has already been said, one of the key approaches I have used here, particularly in Chapter 3, is to seek to break down Wright's scholarship into 'bite-sized chunks' to make it more digestible. Running the risk, as all summaries do, of simplification becoming distortion, this approach has been taken in the hope of providing a framework in which readers can locate and understand more of its distinctive aspects.

The other major approach that I have used is that of recounting story. For instance, in Chapter 2 a certain amount of my own personal experience within British evangelicalism is used to convey a number of pressing theological questions to which Wright's theology has provided compelling answers. In Chapters 4, 5 and 6 this method is used again, in a slightly different manner, to tell the story of the difference that Wright's thought has made to the life of Christ Church, New Malden. Having taken this approach before with my Grove book, *Church Growth Through the Full Welcome of Children: The Sssh Free Church* (itself strongly influenced by Wright's theology), the feedback I received suggested that telling the story of how theology has worked out in practice is an extremely helpful means of conveying this theology.[2] The hope and prayer behind these sections of the book, therefore, is that they will demonstrate, in a vivid and practical manner, the exciting difference that Tom Wright's theology can make to life, worship and mission of the local church. While the context of these stories is that of just one particular parish church within the Church of England, plenty of what is reported here will, I hope, be 'translatable' into other contexts. The final chapter is more general, seeking to outline something of the broader challenge that Wright's theology is presenting to the Church today.

The wider vision behind this book, therefore, lies in my hope that it can play a small role in facilitating Tom Wright's aim of equipping the Church so that it can become more faithful to the Bible's witness and more relevant to the twenty-first-century context in which it is called to minister.[3] Where the more controversial element of its thesis lies is in my conviction that for this to happen the challenge to engage with Wright's theology needs to be heeded most by those who are, at present, more wilfully resisting this engagement. Within the evangelical world, in particular, on both sides of the Atlantic, this lack of engagement is present and based, it seems, on a fear of discovering that some elements within the evangelical tradition may turn out to be far less biblical than has previously been supposed. One of the key aims of this book, therefore, is to encourage, indeed provoke, that proper engagement, not least by showing that there is nothing to fear with legitimacy and everything to be gained by properly engaging with Wright's scholarship. Part of the intention behind its use of elements of personal story is to seek to issue this challenge with humility. These sections aim to model the truth that admission of weaknesses within our understanding and practice as Christians is often the route to locating the resources that God has provided within the Bible for these weaknesses to be addressed.

Thanks are due in a book such as this to many people, starting with Tom Wright himself, both for inspiring its contents and for his helpful comments upon its text. Any remaining mistakes, however, either in the summaries of Tom's work or in the misapplication of its principles within parish life, must be credited to me rather than him! Several members of Christ Church, New Malden have played a similar role, commenting on drafts of the book or inspiring its content through their ministries. As the leaders of the social mission of Christ Church, Sarah Parker and Camilla Pearse have been crucial figures in much of what is reported in Chapter 5. Elizabeth Hill and Trevor Webster have given plenty of encouragement and helpful feedback on the text. In particular, my colleague Helen Hancock has combined a constant enthusiasm, critique and support for this book with the responsibility for devising and implementing many of the developments at Christ Church reported within it. To all of these people I am extremely grateful. Thanks are also due to my father and brothers – Gordon, Martin and Jon Kuhrt – all of whom, from their very different perspectives of Christian ministry, gave me much valuable help and guidance. Last, I need to thank my dear wife Katie and my three wonderful children, Rebecca, James and Abigail, for their patience while Dad had his nose in 'yet another book by Tom Wright'. Not long before I became Vicar of Christ Church, Katie lost her father, Philip King, to cancer. Philip had an immense passion for Christian mission and influence upon its development and so I hope he would have approved of this book. As well as being dedicated to Katie, with much love and gratitude, this book is also written, therefore, in memory of my father-in-law. As Tom Wright would put it (and indeed did put it in an email after Philip's death), 'May he rest in peace and rise in glory!'

Stephen Kuhrt
Christ Church, New Malden
September 2010

Foreword by N. T. Wright

I was surprised and delighted when Stephen Kuhrt told me he was planning to write this book. I have known Stephen for some years, and all that I have heard of his lively church has been a real encouragement. But I hadn't realized the extent to which my own thinking and writing lay behind some of the things he, and his colleagues in mission and ministry, had been attempting.

I have, of course, always hoped and prayed that the work I have done would be a helpful resource for those engaged in the church's front-line activities. I have often spoken of theological scholarship as a kind of scaffolding – not necessarily the sort of thing you want to see when you had hoped to admire a proper building, but necessary from time to time if the building is going to stay in good shape and not be damaged by wind, weather or structural undermining.

There has, of course, been quite a lot of wind, weather and structural undermining in the western Church in recent decades, and I'm glad if my work, along with that of many others, has helped to provide the scaffolding for various parts of the church to repair and rebuild. Something of that is evident in what Stephen is reporting here. But I think there is more as well.

I have had a sense, ever since I embarked on serious research into Jesus himself in the late 1970s – the work that reached its fullest flowering in *Jesus and the Victory of God* (1996) and *The Challenge of Jesus* (1999) – that I was bringing together two quite different worlds which most western Christians had held apart. What was driving me in this was my historical as well as my theological conscience. I couldn't deny the faith I have always held about who Jesus was and is – God's own son, come to rescue the world and launch God's kingdom – without becoming a different person altogether. (Yes, some make that decision, but that wasn't for me.) But nor could I deny, as an ancient historian, that it was important to be able to say with conviction that Jesus really did and said what the Gospels say he did and said. (Yes, this leaves room for questions about details, but the overall picture must be secure, or faith is based on thin air.) As I read, taught, prayed and wrote in this area over many years I had a sense that Jesus was becoming more real, more three-dimensional, quite different in some ways from the 'Jesus' I had grown up with but in other ways richly integrating all sorts of things I had dimly intuited but never quite grasped. This isn't to say I got everything right, but I sensed I was at least on the right track.

In bringing theology and history together I was attempting a harder task than I then realized: I was trying to overcome a big split that has run down the middle of western culture for at least 200 years and quite possibly a lot longer. Many teachers and preachers have thanked me for doing this, enabling them to go about their work not only with a clear conscience but with a far more robust sense of who Jesus actually was. I think that sense of overcoming a split world and a split gospel is at the heart of what Stephen's book is about.

Bringing theology and history together also meant bringing faith and life together. So often western Christians have divided into two camps: those for whom Jesus died for their sins to rescue them from the world altogether, and those for whom Jesus lived to open up a new way of righting the wrongs in the world. This is, if you like, the puzzle of the cross and the kingdom. Some Christians focus on the cross and forget the kingdom; others do the reverse. But the four Gospels bring them together and hold them together. God's kingdom is to come *on earth as in heaven* – but that happens not only through Jesus' life, his healings, teachings, feastings and so on, but supremely through Jesus' death. (And, of course, his resurrection and ascension, the former meaning that God's new world has been launched, the latter meaning that he is now firmly in charge of it.)

This has immediate and urgent relevance to Christian mission and ministry, and Stephen Kuhrt's book shows what happens when you take this vision and give it breath, brains and a budget. It should never have been a matter of *either* telling people that Jesus died so that they could go to heaven *or* urging them to work for better housing, for a cure for AIDS, and for world peace. Both are clearly on God's agenda: they should be on ours as well.

But here comes the next wrinkle. 'Going to heaven' isn't really good enough as a description of the Christian hope. Here Stephen Kuhrt has rightly grasped the vision I outline in my big book *The Resurrection of the Son of God* and the more popular *Surprised by Hope*. 'New heavens and new earth' is what we are promised – and God has already launched that project with Jesus. God's kingdom isn't 'from' this world, but it is certainly *for* this world. Our ultimate hope is to be raised from the dead to share in the running of God's new creation. *And all that we do by way of Christian, Spirit-led work in the present is a genuine foretaste of that.* When we work for the poor, or for victims of a disaster, or whatever, we are not oiling the wheels of a machine that will then drive over a cliff. We are not 'building the kingdom' by our own efforts. Only God does that. But we are building *for* the kingdom. And that has to be done, as Stephen and his colleagues are attempting to do, in very practical ways at the local level.

Two other large areas go closely with all this. The first is the question of how we read St Paul. Here again I have been determined to let Paul speak from his own first-century context rather than insist that he be made to answer to the sixteenth-century questions, which shaped the Reformation, in their own terms. This has been difficult and sometimes controversial. From time to time people accuse me of no longer 'preaching the gospel'. Stephen Kuhrt has shown, I think, that this simply isn't the case. When we announce that the crucified and risen Jesus is the world's true Lord, we *are* 'preaching the gospel'. People are simultaneously called to faith (by which they will be justified – will be declared by God to be 'in the right') and called to active service and obedience (by which, through them, God will continue his work of putting the world right). Paul has for a long time been a closed book to some churches and a favourite but misunderstood hero for others. I have tried to set out a bigger picture of what he was all about, and I'm delighted Stephen and others have found this fruitful in evangelism and pastoral work.

The final area is that of the sacraments. If heaven and earth, theology and history, and faith and life go together more closely than we had imagined, we shouldn't be surprised if sometimes God chooses to act, to be present to save and heal, in and through symbolic parts of the world of space, time and matter. Again, the western Church has found it difficult to articulate and experience this without becoming too 'spiritual' on the one hand or too 'material' on the other. Hence, alas, some of our deepest divisions. I hope that the experience of

Stephen and others like him will begin to show that these divisions are based on an unnecessary and diminished reading of our core texts, and that there are better and more creative ways forward.

In all this, of course, my main aim has been to help people read, preach and live the Bible more thoroughly, faithfully and excitedly. Stephen Kuhrt has clearly been doing this in his own ministry, and I hope and pray that, through his fine (and flattering) study of my work and its effects, many others will come to find it too. My thanks, then, to Stephen himself, to those who have worked with him, and to the publishers for adding yet another 'Tom Wright' book to their list, albeit this time by someone else!

The Right Reverend Professor N. T. Wright, DD
University of St Andrews

1

The career of Tom Wright: emergence, scholarship and non-engagement

In order to understand the emergence of Tom Wright as a major figure within the current Christian world, a certain amount of background is helpful. Nicholas Thomas Wright was born in Morpeth in Northumberland in the north of England in 1948. Brought up within what he has described as 'middle Anglicanism', Wright's first sense of a calling to full-time Christian ministry came at the age of just seven or eight. He initially assumed that this would lead him into parish ministry, but the course of Wright's vocation started to change in the early 1970s while reading Classics at Exeter College, Oxford. Active within the Oxford Inter-Collegiate Christian Union and strongly influenced at that stage by Calvinism, Wright's first publication came as an undergraduate. Along with three other students, he produced *The Grace of God in the Gospel*, published by the Banner of Truth Trust.[1]

A more crucial moment for his future, however, was the point during those years when Wright heard a talk by John Wenham on the need for Christians committed to the authority of Scripture to enter the world of biblical and theological scholarship. In response to this clarification of his vocation, Wright's ordination, as an Anglican deacon in 1975 and priest in 1976, was followed over the next 20 years by a series of university posts in Oxford, Cambridge and Montreal. Initially focused upon Pauline theology, the subject of his doctoral thesis, it was during the late 1970s that the distinctive nature of Wright's understanding of Pauline theology started to form. This thesis was built upon, but in some ways radically challenged, the work of E. P. Sanders, whose 1977 book *Paul and Palestinian Judaism* is regarded as the start of the 'new perspective' on Paul.[2] Sometime later Wright's focus then broadened as 'the historical Jesus' joined with

1

Paul to become his second main area of research.[3] Identified during this period as a rising evangelical scholar, Wright served for a time as Secretary of the Council of Latimer House, a research centre established by Jim Packer and others to advance the cause of evangelical scholarship within the Church of England. Around this time his contributions to the development of evangelical Anglicanism included writing, along with Michael Sadgrove, a chapter on the meaning of salvation (entitled 'Jesus Christ the only Saviour') within the first of the three preparatory books written for the second National Evangelical Congress held at Nottingham in 1977.[4] In 1980 Wright also published a Latimer Study entitled *Evangelical Anglican Identity: The Connection Between Bible, Gospel and Church*, partly based on research into issues of evangelical Anglican identity that he conducted at the request of the Church of England Evangelical Council.[5]

At this stage of his career, the results of Wright's biblical scholarship were still largely limited to articles within academic journals that did not reach a wider audience.[6] An exception to this was *Small Faith, Great God*, produced in 1978 and based upon sermons that Wright had delivered to student Christian groups in Oxford.[7] Awareness of Wright's biblical scholarship among a broader evangelical constituency was raised when he produced a commentary on *Colossians and Philemon* for the Tyndale series in 1986.[8] Two years later, in 1988, he produced, with Stephen Neill, an updated version of Neill's *The Interpretation of the New Testament*. Originally covering the period between 1861 and 1961, the book's overview of New Testament scholarship was extended to 1986.[9] Generally speaking, however, during the 1970s and 1980s Wright was relatively unknown within the wider Christian world and the impact of his scholarship was yet to be felt.

This started to change from the early to mid 1990s, partly as a result of Wright's move to more high-profile posts within the Church of England. He was appointed Dean of Lichfield in 1994, Canon Theologian of Westminster Abbey in 2000, and Bishop of Durham in 2003. Of even greater significance to his profile was the fact that his previous 20 years of research now started to bear fruit in an increasingly prolific production of books that brought Wright's scholarship, quite suddenly, to the attention of a much wider range of people than had previously been the case. Having launched his multi-volume series *Christian Origins and the Question of God* in 1992, it was publication of the second volume, *Jesus and the Victory of God* in 1996 that signalled the turning point here.[10] Accompanied by its more popular versions, *The Original Jesus* in 1996 and *The Challenge of Jesus* in 1999,[11] these books resulted in an increasing number of Christians, particularly clergy, becoming aware that something decisively new was being said about Jesus.

Initially what made the largest impact here was Wright's claim that first-century Israel understood herself to be still in a state of exile, and his presentation of Jesus as an eschatological prophet proclaiming the end of this exile. At this stage Wright was seen within the Christian world primarily as an academic with a gift for communication, and the emergence of his thought was initially regarded with favour by most evangelical Christians. While his views on 'Israel's continuing exile' and his rather different interpretation of Jesus' parables did cause some 'eyebrows to be raised', most evangelicals were very happy to see the confident challenge he was making to the scepticism of other writers on Jesus. These included pseudo-scholars such as Barbara Thiering, A. N. Wilson and Jack Spong, to whom Wright responded with *Who was Jesus?* in 1992, and the reductionist 'Jesus seminar' in America.[12] Those within the more academic world, whose suppositions Wright was also challenging, on the other hand, were inclined to see him as a rather eccentric churchman whose 'interesting ideas' needed taking with a rather large 'pinch of salt'.[13]

Things changed further, particularly within the evangelical world, as Wright's subsequent publications began to bring his distinctive views on eschatology (the Christian hope) to greater prominence. These were anticipated in his Grove book *New Heavens, New Earth* of 1999, but it was in *The Resurrection of the Son of God* in 2003 that Wright produced the weightiest academic work yet seen on the resurrection.[14] His views were further popularized by *Surprised by Hope* in 2007.[15] These works started to clarify the link that Wright had established between the resurrection, a 'new heavens and new earth' eschatology and the radical agenda that both of these established for the Church. Significantly, this agenda contained some key elements very different from those traditionally promoted by evangelicals.[16]

Throughout much of the 1990s, certainly in terms of popular consciousness, Wright's work on Paul remained largely in the background. This was mainly because his volume on Paul in the *Christian Origins and the Question of God* series was awaiting its turn to be written.[17] While his Tyndale commentary on *Colossians and Philemon* had been produced in 1986, circulation of his detailed essays on Pauline theology were still mainly limited to academic circles. This included the volume in which a number of these essays were published in 1991, *The Climax of the Covenant*.[18] It was the publication of *What St Paul Really Said* in 1997[19] that really raised a more popular consciousness of Wright's Pauline theology, particularly in the USA, as his distinctive understanding of 'justification by faith' started to become clear. Publication of his major commentary on Romans in *The New Interpreters Bible* in 2002 and then *Paul: Fresh Perspectives* (in the USA the title was *Paul in Fresh Perspective*) in 2005 contributed further to the profile of his Pauline theology.[20] The latter was particularly important for drawing out the political significance of Paul's theology. Wright's understanding of 'justification', meanwhile, provoked responses from a number of US websites, and eventually, in 2008, a book by John Piper, *The Future of Justification: A Response to N. T. Wright*.[21] Wright himself responded to Piper's book with *Justification: God's Plan and Paul's Vision* in 2009.[22]

Running alongside his more academic works, from the 1990s onwards Wright produced a number of more popular level books. These included *New Tasks for a Renewed Church* in 1992, *The Lord and his Prayer* in 1996, *For All God's Worth* in 1997 and *Holy Communion for Amateurs* in 1999 (later retitled *The Meal Jesus Gave Us*).[23] In 2001 he began a series of popular commentaries called the *For Everyone* series; by 2008 this had covered every book of the New Testament other than the non-Pauline epistles (with the exception of Hebrews) and Revelation.[24] Later on these were edited to form a number of guides to facilitate their further study.[25] *Simply Christian* was produced in 2006 for those exploring the claims of Christianity, and Wright's reflection on a number of other areas resulted in the publication of *Scripture and the Authority of God* (2005), *Evil and the Justice of God* (2006), *Judas and the Gospel of Jesus* (2006) and *Virtue Reborn* (2010).[26]

Alongside this prolific output,[27] Wright found the time to play an important role within the Church of England and Anglican Communion, contributing to a number of its commissions and reports. This role increased once Wright became Bishop of Durham, particularly in regard to the formation of *The Windsor Report*, as differences regarding homosexuality began to tear the Anglican Communion apart.[28] As a senior bishop in the Church of England,

Wright made a number of important speeches in the House of Lords (the second chamber of the UK Houses of Parliament) as well as the Church of England's General Synod. Wright also played a significant role in the formation of Fulcrum, a movement launched in 2003 to renew the evangelical centre of the Church of England, the context in which I personally got to know him.[29] Important though all this direct work within church leadership has been, Wright's primary calling has remained that of providing the Church with the fruits of biblical scholarship. This priority guided Wright's decision in 2010 to resign as Bishop of Durham to take up his current post as Professor of New Testament and Early Christianity at the University of St Andrews in Scotland.

It is clear, then, that in under two decades, Tom Wright has moved from being virtually unknown to being arguably the most influential biblical scholar in the English-speaking world today. The sheer scale and breadth of Wright's work, his commitment to providing for popular as well as academic audiences, and his dual role for much of this time as both church leader and academic, have all been vital factors contributing to this outcome. Wright's wider interests in walking, sport and particularly music, his gift for humour and openness about his commitment to his family and friends have also played a significant role here in facilitating the ease with which he has been able to communicate his theology within his books, lectures, interviews and broadcasts.[30]

All this background is given, however, to make a claim that some might then find surprising: that proper engagement with Tom Wright's scholarship within the Christian world is not nearly as advanced as it should be. This is true at both ends of the theological spectrum. As part of my training for ordination into the Church of England between 2000 and 2003, I sat the BA in Theology at Oxford University. Having already read a good amount of what Wright had published at that stage, I was both surprised and disappointed at the low level of interest in this scholarship by the faculty's lecturers. To an overwhelming extent, they had not engaged with Wright's thought and largely remained within old and rather tired paradigms for understanding the New Testament. These included assumptions concerning the essential unreliability of the Gospels as testimony concerning the historical Jesus, the implausibility of Jesus himself possessing any messianic self-understanding, the political quietism of Acts and Paul's letters, the lack of 'atonement theology' in the Gospels, particularly Luke, the title 'Christ' possessing little or no messianic significance within Paul's theology, and Christian eschatology meaning an expectation of the imminent end of the world. All these assumptions needed urgent reconsideration in the light of Wright's work, and yet there was no sign of this happening. The impression I gained during my time in Oxford was that the study of Wright's scholarship was avoided because of its potential for collapsing so much 'critical' thinking on the New Testament that had achieved 'foundational' status.[31]

More disturbing, however, is my impression that this lack of engagement with the theology of Tom Wright is just as true within the majority of evangelical churches in Britain. Within many such churches, pleasure at Wright's defence of credal orthodoxy, particularly the physical resurrection of Jesus and also his maintenance of the Church's tradition on the question of homosexual practice, has combined with most of their members failing to 'get it' when it comes to understanding the distinctiveness of his overall theology. As a result of this, they too have largely remained within their existing paradigms for understanding both the New Testament and their Christian faith.

The most obvious example of this is in relation to eschatology. Here, even among those who have read some of Wright's works, 'going to heaven when you die' has usually remained their understanding of the Christian hope, with all its serious consequences for the agenda of their churches. Wright himself has admitted that this understanding is so deeply entrenched within western Christianity that he sometimes despairs of ever being able to change it.[32] This is particularly true of evangelical churches where the assumption about the orthodoxy of understanding 'heaven' as 'the Christian's true home' remains extremely well established. Rather than being a rejection of Wright's understanding of 'new heavens, new earth', it is more a case of the distinctiveness of this view of the Christian hope, and especially its radical implications for the Christian agenda, not yet being heard.

Where clergy have made some progress in grappling with this, and other aspects of Wright's thought, there often remains a reluctance or insecurity as to whether to share this theology with congregations and allow it to change the way in which church is 'done'. On a number of occasions I have met clergy who have admitted to finding Wright's books extremely enriching and compelling, particularly in the way that his writing has opened up the Bible to them and stimulated their personal devotion. Once the conversation has progressed to how this theology might lead to change in the agenda of our churches, however, it has usually become more anxious and evasive. This is perhaps in part through an uncertainty about how to apply Wright's theology. More often, though, it seems to be prompted by concern about the appropriateness of this suggestion – almost as though what is acceptable for 'consenting vicars' to do in the privacy of their studies should not be allowed any further! Where a link with my Oxford lecturers may exist is in a fear, especially among more conservative evangelicals, of what genuine engagement with the scholarship of Tom Wright might lead to: namely, a great deal of foundational church practice, previously assumed as 'biblical', having to be reviewed and possibly changed.

Even where Tom Wright has received explicit criticism, it could be argued that a proper engagement with his scholarship has still failed to happen. Wright himself makes this claim in his response to the criticism that he has received from John Piper and others in regard to his understanding of the Pauline concept of 'justification'. Piper's book *The Future of Justification: A Response to N. T. Wright* was published in 2008 and largely consists of a detailed examination of Pauline texts with the aim of showing why Wright was incorrect in his claims about how 'justification' should be understood.[33] Much of Wright's counter-response in *Justification: God's Plan and Paul's Vision* then focused upon the extent to which Piper and other critics had failed to engage with the vital foundations of Wright's different reading of these texts. Key to this is the importance Wright lays upon the story of Israel in the Old Testament being allowed to carry its full weight in the formation of New Testament theology, rather than being reduced to a mere backdrop providing some 'types' and prophecies. Having failed to pay proper attention to Wright's emphasis upon the cosmic scope of God's project of salvation, the resulting nature of God's covenant plan, the significance of Jesus as Israel's Messiah and the role of the Holy Spirit, Piper was then unable to see how these factors had led to Wright's different understanding. Piper, rather than engage with the alternative paradigm that Wright has proposed for understanding Pauline theology, had critiqued its end result from the perspective of his own unquestioned paradigm, leading him to make little sense of these proposals. The problem, as Wright asserted, was that Piper had not so much disagreed with his work as completely ignored it.[34]

Something very similar was evident in 2007. Wright was at the centre of a controversy over his critical review of a book called *Pierced for Our Transgressions* by Steve Jeffrey, Mike Ovey and Andrew Sach. This book formed a strong defence of the biblical nature of the doctrine of penal substitution and was written against the background of an increasing number of evangelicals being ready to question aspects of this understanding of the atonement.[35] While affirming the book's several merits and stating his own defence of penal substitution, Wright's overall tone was extremely critical, calling the book 'deeply, profoundly and disturbingly unbiblical'. The basis of this accusation was, again, the claim that it had ignored *the story* of Israel and restricted the role of the Old Testament to providing some sacrificial 'types' for Jesus' atoning death. This failure to understand the death of Jesus as the climax of the Bible's entire narrative, Wright argued, had resulted in the book's particular marginalization of the Gospel narratives and their vital role in giving a fully biblical and rounded understanding of the atonement.[36]

Wright was honest in his review about the personal frustration that he felt about *Pierced for Our Transgressions*. This was because all the omissions mentioned above reflected the refusal, or inability, of the authors to engage with Wright's own substantial writing on the death of Jesus, particularly within Chapter 12 of his *Jesus and the Victory of God* (the fullest exposition ever of Jesus' self-understanding in relation to the Isaianic servant) and Chapter 3 of his *Evil and the Justice of God*. While *Pierced for Our Transgressions* does occasionally refer to aspects of Wright's scholarship, it is usually with a degree of ambivalence, resulting from its writers' essential unwillingness to engage with the claims for understanding the biblical material that Wright sets out.[37] Once again, the problem is emphatically not that Wright's arguments have been outlined and then rejected; it is that such an engagement has been completely avoided.

This reluctance within the evangelical world to acknowledge the importance of Tom Wright's scholarship has also been evident at an institutional level. The first time I heard Wright speak was in London in January 1996 at the Second Evangelical Anglican Leaders Conference.

This conference, like its predecessor a year earlier, was called by the evangelical bishops of the Church of England in an effort to encourage unity, purpose and dialogue among evangelical Anglicans. As part of this, Tom Wright, then still Dean of Lichfield, was invited to give a Bible reading on Luke 24, and then conduct a dialogue with the conservative evangelical Paul Gardner on its contents. Some present regarded the dialogue as somewhat 'donnish', but others were intrigued as Gardner questioned aspects of Wright's theology, such as his thesis that first-century Israel understood herself to be in a continuing state of exile, and Wright defended and gave further explanation of his understanding. At that point an encouragement of engagement with Wright's emerging scholarship seemed very much on the evangelical agenda.

Since that point, the very opposite has seemed to be true. Subsequent national evangelical conferences in the Church of England have very deliberately excluded Wright from speaking. For example, in 2003 the Church of England Evangelical Council (CEEC) called the fourth National Evangelical Anglican Congress (NEAC4) at Blackpool. Previous NEACs, particularly Keele in 1967 and Nottingham in 1977, had been significant for the development of evangelical Anglicanism in the UK; as mentioned earlier, a young Tom Wright had co-authored a chapter to the first volume of the pre-Nottingham trilogy *Obeying Christ in a Changing World* edited by John Stott.[38] Stott summed up the first three NEACs as being about 'Involvement' in the Church of England (Keele), 'Hermeneutics' (Nottingham) and 'Integration' (Caister, NEAC3 in 1988), and this revealed much about their desire to engage in areas that evangelicals had previously avoided.[39] By 2003 and NEAC4, however, the CEEC (by then chaired by Paul Gardner) had a more reactionary agenda, the reassertion of traditional evangelical approaches to 'Bible, Cross and Mission' being seen as the priority.[40] Tom Wright was invited to attend and provided with a speaker's badge, but was not asked to speak, while few if any of those who did address the three-day conference made any real engagement with his theology. By NEAC5 in 2008, held in London as a one-day 'consultation' and now generally regarded as a disaster, there was no expectation that the CEEC would either ask Wright to speak or engage with his thought.

Something similar occurred in 2010 in preparation for the 'Lausanne' Congress in South Africa. The original International Congress on

World Evangelization at Lausanne in 1974 was chaired by Billy Graham, with John Stott once again playing a key role.[41] Part of the significance of the Congress was its role in establishing the commitment of evangelicals to social action alongside evangelism, an emphasis that the subsequent 'Lausanne' movement sought to safeguard.[42] It might have been expected that Wright would be invited to speak in South Africa in 2010, given the very strong biblical basis for holistic mission that he had by this stage established, particularly through his development of the implications of a 'new heavens, new earth' eschatology. Once again, however, Wright was invited to attend but not to speak, an invitation he this time declined. Some of those attending the UK delegates' meeting in London raised questions about the lack of engagement with Tom Wright's theology and the corresponding reliance of those who spoke on rather dated 1970s models to support the need for holistic mission. A somewhat evasive public response to these questions indicated the overall reluctance of Lausanne to engage with Wright's theology.

As a result of all this, Tom Wright could be described as currently occupying rather similar positions within two 'worlds', which are normally some distance from one another but which, by his very person, he brings together: the world of academic biblical scholarship and the world of evangelical Christianity. In both areas, the range of Wright's work has been immense. Within both, however, paradoxically this productivity is combined with a very strong reluctance to engage with Wright's work; chiefly, because of a fear of what foundational 'truths' might then be questioned and potentially changed. Perhaps it would be more accurate to describe this as an unwillingness *to allow engagement*, since this reticence is not nearly so strong among other groups of Christians – university students, for example, and many 'ordinary' clergy and lay people. There are stories from the deeply conservative Anglican diocese of Sydney, Australia, for instance, of theological students reading Wright's books in their study rooms without their tutor's knowledge! Within 'critical Oxford' a number of theological students I knew during my time there also felt a similar reluctance to admit that they had consulted the work of one regarded by *their* tutors as a 'fundamentalist'.

Such factors mean that it is no easy task for those living in either 'world' to access the full scope of Wright's work and explore its implications. The reason for this book is to encourage such exploration so that the exciting thought of Tom Wright can contribute to the renewal of both 'worlds': biblical scholarship and evangelical Christianity. An even greater and perhaps rather idealistic hope is that it might help Wright's thought to play a role in the end of their separation.

2

Theological questions awaiting an answer . . .

———•◆•———

As mentioned in the Preface, part of this book's approach involves using story as a means of giving readers further access to the scholarship of Tom Wright. In this chapter that story is largely personal, as I seek to outline a number of issues that puzzled me in my earlier Christian life and were eventually resolved with the immense help of the theology of Tom Wright. The questionability of this approach is obvious. As well as the risk of being somewhat self-indulgent, the questions and issues that I faced growing up within the Christian faith will not be identical to those of every reader. My experience of being brought up in a clergy family, in the centre and then the south of England, completely immersed within the evangelical Anglican tradition, is, I am aware, probably far from typical.

However, I have persisted with the personal story approach of this chapter for two reasons. First, recounting personal story makes it easier to give readers access to the issues raised in this chapter than presenting these issues in more abstract form. Second, I do believe that mine is a story that points to issues common enough within the evangelical tradition for its narration to be helpful and worth telling. While it represents an essentially Anglican and certainly very English experience of evangelical Christianity, my expectation is that plenty within it will resonate with the experience of many readers.

Growing up 'evangelical' from the early 1970s onwards was on the whole a hugely positive experience. The enthusiasm and energy of the large and vibrant churches we attended for life-changing and relevant Christianity was something that I found exciting and attractive. As I grew older, committed youth leaders and fantastic summer camps played an important role in my Christian nurture, modelling a passion for truth and a commitment to my development that made a large impact. Never really knowing a time when I didn't believe in Jesus, on such a camp during the summer of 1984, at the age of 15 I made a decisive personal commitment to own this faith for myself. Ups and downs in my spiritual life inevitably followed, but the evangelical tradition, having brought me to faith, then nurtured most of my formation and vocation, chiefly through the opportunities it swiftly provided for me to be involved in youth work and mission. Evangelical Christian books, particularly by authors such as John Stott and Michael Green, and regular attendance at events such as Spring Harvest, were also important in my Christian development. This input played the decisive role in the calling that gradually clarified within me to serve God, first as a Christian schoolteacher and later as a clergyman.

Looking back, therefore, I am immensely grateful for all that over 40 years within the evangelical tradition has given me. Throughout these years it has been very obvious to me that I have been living within a tradition with numerous strengths, particularly in the desire to take the Bible seriously and teach its contents faithfully. Within this context, evangelicalism seemed particularly 'at home' when it came to explaining certain themes, namely the identity and uniqueness of Jesus, the 'once and for all' nature of his atoning death, the priority of God's grace and the need to make a response of faith, including a changed lifestyle. All these things I was taught to place great value upon and still do.

Even at a relatively young age, however, I started to become aware that there were other areas where the evangelical tradition possessed less confidence. While some of these appeared 'theological' and others more 'practical', I can now see how entwined they were. What follows is not an exhaustive statement of weaknesses within the evangelical tradition; it concentrates on those issues that I became aware of and for me at least eventually found a great deal of resolution, principally through engagement with Tom Wright's theology.

The nature of the Christian hope

The most obvious of these issues was with regard to the Christian hope. In the evangelical tradition the focus of this hope was so assumed that it was rarely seen to require explanation: 'going to heaven when we die'. Like many children, the reality of death was something that became apparent to me from about the age of six or seven. This was exacerbated by a Cold War perspective that declared that the world could easily end at any moment at the press of a button! In response to these anxieties, the message I received from my evangelical tradition was that I needn't be worried about death because, if I placed my trust in Jesus, he would 'prepare a place for me in heaven'. Other than the addition of a counterpart for 'heaven' in 'hell', this understanding of the Christian future hope that I received as a child was subject to very little amendment from my tradition as I grew older.

With 'going to heaven when we die' thus established as the *nature* of the Christian hope, it appeared quite logical that the greatest urgency in terms of theology was establishing clarity over the means by which this 'entry into heaven' could be gained. Here the answer, especially on Christian summer camps, was very clear: by placing our faith in the free gift of Jesus and the sufficiency of his atoning death. While plenty of other benefits to being a Christian were presented and embodied, it was quite hard to see how any of them were more important than guaranteeing that crucial 'place in heaven'. As a consequence, it was easy to see why the greatest urgency in terms of evangelical *mission* was placed on 'getting people into heaven' by encouraging others to recognize and accept this 'free gift' as well.

One problem that occurred to me as I entered my teens was the difficulty of attracting people to this message unless they were particularly concerned with the question of what would happen to them after death. Most outside the Church seemed to share the assumption that what Christianity had to offer chiefly centred on this question of our individual destination, and in an increasingly postmodern culture such reassurance was seen as necessary for some but not important for others. Circumstances could change, of course, making this issue more pressing. But tales of people such as Steve McQueen, who engaged with Christianity as he neared death, then 'making a commitment', only tended to reinforce the idea that guaranteeing that individual place in heaven was what Christianity was essentially all about.[1]

Significantly, however, for the majority of those I saw becoming Christians, gaining 'a place in heaven' didn't seem to be the primary factor in attracting them. For most of them it was encountering something that made sense in the *present* reality of their life that seemed to be more important. This often appeared to be meaningful incorporation within a Christian community, with or without an obvious awareness of God's Spirit transforming their life. Understanding 'eternal life' as beginning in the present and the Spirit's role as a 'down-payment' made some connection here. But a major disjuncture nonetheless seemed to exist between what was presented as the nature of the Christian hope and what people were receiving most from following Jesus. This lack of connection was summed up, rather than resolved, when I heard Cliff Richard promoting Christianity as not just being 'pie in the sky when you die' but 'cake on your plate while you wait'. Other than the explanation that release from the fear of death brought the liberation to 'have life in abundance' now, not much integration was made between what was presented as our 'future hope' and our Christian life in the present.

Another problem that increasingly occurred to me in my late teens was to do with the tentative relationship that 'going to heaven when you die' appeared to have to the biblical and credal material concerning our future hope. This was particularly true in regard to 'the second coming of Jesus' and 'the resurrection of the dead'. I got used to affirming these doctrines through regularly reciting the Apostles' and Nicene Creeds in services at church. However, it gradually became apparent to me that these beliefs had very little impact upon the way in which the Christian hope was being presented. 'The resurrection of the dead' was largely reduced to being a metaphor for 'the hope of heaven', with an occasional emphasis on the fact that when we got 'to heaven' we would receive new bodies. With 'heaven' frequently described as 'our real home', it was also rather difficult to see where 'the second coming of Jesus' connected with this, particularly given the little emphasis within my very English brand of evangelicalism upon a belief in a 'rapture'. As a result, the way in which all these various 'pieces' of Christian eschatology fitted together was left pretty much unexplained. The 2001 hymn 'In Christ alone' by Stuart Townend and Keith Getty has become quite a classic in recent years but the lack of resolution to its final line ("til Christ returns or calls me home') reflects this continuing uncertainty. As I grew older, my confusion about the nature of the Christian hope was reinforced by encountering passages, particularly in Matthew's Gospel, that *did* refer to 'the kingdom of heaven' but were clearly understanding the concept of 'heaven' in a rather different way from its most common use within my tradition.

The significance of the resurrection of Jesus

Linked to this was a similar uncertainty that I started to see within the evangelical tradition with regard to the resurrection of Jesus himself. This might initially seem a staggering claim, given the very strong defence of the physical resurrection of Jesus often mounted by evangelicals against 'more liberal' Christians. What I began to realize, however, was the extent to which evangelicals were more comfortable presenting 'the evidence for the resurrection' than really reflecting on its theological significance. With the death of Jesus firmly at the centre of evangelical theology and presented as the sole means by which people could 'get into heaven', the significance of Jesus' resurrection appeared limited to the supporting role of 'showing that the cross had worked'.

There was an illustration of this in 1984. The newly appointed Bishop of Durham, David Jenkins, caused immense controversy when he questioned, among other things, whether the resurrection of Jesus should be regarded as 'physical'. This was immediately met with considerable indignation by evangelicals and a very strong defence of the 'physical resurrection of Jesus' from the pulpits of many such churches across the UK. The evangelical constituency was speedily provided with *The Authentic Jesus* by John Stott (1985), which rebutted Jenkins on both this issue and other beliefs about which he had expressed scepticism, such as the Virgin Birth.[2] What this incident did not provoke to any great extent was genuine reflection upon the *theological* significance of the physical resurrection of Jesus, which would, as we will see later, have responded far more effectively to Jenkins' scepticism. Interestingly, and with hindsight a greater amount of reflection on the resurrection could have spoken very prophetically (and supportively) into the political agenda that Jenkins was also pursuing at the time, as he supported Britain's coal miners in their protracted industrial dispute with Margaret Thatcher's Conservative government. This sort of reflection, however, was at the time not really on the agenda of evangelicals; the importance of the physical resurrection of Jesus was defended rather than explored or particularly linked to the nature of our future hope.

To be fair, some connections were made between the physical resurrection of Jesus and the nature of the hope of both Christ's followers and the world. John Stott wrote in *The Authentic Jesus* of the Christian hope being not of an ethereal 'heaven' but a 'regenerated universe'.[3] Such points, however, were not particularly 'heard' by evangelicals mainly because there was no energy or desire among their leaders to challenge the prevailing notion of 'heaven' as the Christian's final destination. All this left me quietly confused, as a 1980s teenager, about what all the fuss had been about. If 'going to heaven when we die' *is* the nature of the Christian hope, I allowed myself to ponder, what is the *theological* problem with believing that Jesus did the same? 'Because the Bible says that Jesus rose from the dead, and believing in the physical resurrection of Jesus shows that we trust the Bible!', seemed the best that my evangelical tradition could muster in response. Over a decade would pass before I discovered a far more compelling and biblical answer.

The lack of a convincing theological basis for holistic mission

Running alongside these questions was another seemingly separate issue that increasingly began to trouble me from my late teens and early twenties: the theological basis for a holistic approach to Christian mission. Having grown up within a fairly comfortable middle-class setting in a suburb of south London, I became rather urgently aware of this issue when I became involved in inner-city mission through an annual children's holiday club, which took place in the more deprived parts of Islington in north London. It was clear to me within this context that our mission agenda had to be to respond to the whole needs of those children and adults to whom we were seeking to minister. Beyond this, it clarified my conviction that Christian mission had also to attend to the causes of such deprivation as well as to its results. In the years that followed, therefore, I became steadily convinced that issues of politics and justice, and also care for the environment, had to form just as important a part of the Christian agenda for mission as personal evangelism.

I was uncomfortably aware, however, that I had reached these conclusions *despite* my evangelical heritage rather than because of it. The hope of 'going to heaven when we die' appeared, after all, to signal a very clear priority for evangelism, ahead of any radically social, environmental or political agenda. While few evangelicals I met were actually opposed to Christian social action, the disdain one still heard for 'liberals' with their 'social gospel' and the clear dislike for Christians being 'too political' suggested that the attitude towards such mission was at best ambivalent. I was reassured to only a limited extent by the work that John Stott and others had done to restore social justice to a position of importance within Christian mission through their writings, action and production of the Lausanne Covenant (particularly its section 5 on 'Social Responsibility'). This was because despite this work, a satisfying and fully integrated biblical model for the equality of evangelism and social action within Christian mission still remained elusive. From this basis, both Lausanne and Billy Graham concluded that evangelism must still remain the primary task of the church.[4] Stott's writings, while generally seeking to resist this conclusion, continued to betray something of a struggle to explain why Christian social responsibility should have equal importance alongside evangelism.[5] Models developed by others that described the partnership of evangelism and social action being 'like the two blades of a pair of scissors or the two wings of a bird' suggested a similar struggle to supply an integrated theological rationale to satisfy these instincts about the importance of holistic mission.[6]

This continuing theological uncertainty resulted in a clear priority for evangelism over social action within the evangelical churches I encountered. I was aware of Pentecostal and charismatic Christians, with their greater emphasis upon removing Satan from his 'strongholds' on earth, making a greater use of both the Gospels and 'the kingdom of God' to support their holistic mission. However, even here a fundamental lack of integration was suggested in the readiness to describe the major social impact of famous revivals as 'the fruits of evangelistic endeavour' and to speak of 'the supernatural expectancy that should *accompany* the preaching of the gospel'. Reducing social change to being 'an outcome of the gospel', with an inevitable plea for patience over progress, stood in stark contrast with the urgency presented for evangelism. This reinforced the sense that the social mission of the church possessed a very secondary status.

What increasingly concerned me, as someone very interested in history, was the way in which this attitude seemed to back up the claim of Karl Marx when he described religion, including Christianity, as the 'opiate of the people'. More than once I heard evangelicals quoting Jesus' saying that 'the poor will always be with you' (John 12.8) as a way of relativizing the need for an active social mission. Steadily more aware of the overwhelmingly middle-class and affluent nature of much of English evangelicalism, this 'convenient truth' concerning the movement's missional priorities began to trouble me deeply. As yet, however, I lacked much theology to support this critique, beyond the very different example of how Jesus chose to spend his time.

The moment that encapsulated this conundrum was when I made a comment to a young clergyman that social care and political justice should have equal priority to personal evangelism because this was what Jesus modelled. 'What is going to last?' was his curt reply, implying that since this was only individual souls, the agenda of saving these souls had to have priority.[7] At that stage I was completely unaware of the way in which, as I would later discover thanks to Tom Wright, that curate's question was completely the *right* one, albeit with a very different answer from the one we both supposed. Having been taught that the Christian hope was about 'going to heaven when you die', I was completely unaware of the process of 'unlearning' I would have to undergo regarding this understanding of eschatology and its resulting implications for Christian mission.

Evangelical treatments of sin and evil

Linked to this area was my growing awareness of the weaknesses in how evangelicals were apt to understand and present sin.[8] This again might seem rather strange, since acknowledgement of the reality and gravity of sin is usually seen as a major strength of evangelicalism. It was more liberal Christians, I was taught to believe, who had 'a weak doctrine of sin' and this was chiefly responsible for their failure to possess beliefs similar to evangelicals about grace and the atonement.

What became apparent to me, however, was that evangelicalism was geared more towards understanding and making sense of *personal* sin rather than anything of a collective or structural nature. Standard evangelical explanations of how the death of Jesus brought us forgiveness, for instance, tended to present the idea of sin as something that was essentially *individual*, since this understanding appeared to fit best with the idea of its transfer onto Jesus. This was reinforced by the weekly confession present in most of the Anglican services I attended, and in turn produced an understanding of repentance that while done corporately seemed chiefly about acknowledging this state of personal sin before God in order to be released from it. Like many worshippers, I found this process extremely helpful in leading me to acknowledge my overall need for God's grace and to seek his forgiveness for the personal sins of which I was guilty.

The problem lay in my increasing realization that many of the most damaging forms of sin and evil afflicting the world were those of a structural and collective nature. This appeared particularly obvious in relation to those structures of wealth and power that contributed to most of the inequality, oppression and poverty I saw happening within the world. While there was complete agreement from the evangelical tradition that these things were the result of sin, the overwhelming emphasis upon sin as something personal meant that the need for repentance for our part within more collective sins tended to be somewhat downplayed. It became clear to me that evangelicalism had much more to say about decisions regarding personal morality than about those relating to, for instance, ethical consumption or investment. Playing the National Lottery and 'sleeping around' were therefore very definitely wrong; speculating with people's futures in the stock market, however, or investing money in exploitative companies and building up vast amounts of wealth and possessions were just part of life, and rarely, if ever, called to repentance.

Very suddenly the dominance within evangelical churches of those from more affluent backgrounds and the relative absence of less well-off people had a rather disturbing explanation. Rather than being 'good news for the poor', the primary emphasis within evangelicalism on the need for the removal of guilt from personal sin was actually far better news for the rich, even if some change in personal lifestyle was then expected. Harshly put, if we as evangelicals managed to have our guilt dealt with while carrying on with much the same lifestyle as other wealthy westerners, we could be seen as 'having it sorted'! Rather than pushing me in any way towards a more liberal stance on sin, these thoughts and questions made it clear to me that a far more thorough and biblical treatment of sin, evil and therefore 'repentance' was urgently needed.

Evangelical treatments of the atonement

These thoughts led me, in turn, to a number of searching questions about the most cherished doctrine within evangelicalism – the atonement and specifically penal substitution. Since any questioning of this doctrine tended to be associated with a liberal denial of the reality of sin, the gravity of God's wrath, judgement and the 'once and for all' sufficiency of Jesus' saving death, this required a certain nerve! More than once my questions provoked considerable anger and the suggestion that I was undermining the essence of the gospel.

However, it was increasingly apparent to me that the slickness of many presentations of penal substitution was directly related to some of the problems reported in the previous section. The sole emphasis on 'substitution' in the death of Jesus and the close connection made between this and God 'imputing' Christ's righteousness to us (presented as a central part of the doctrine of 'justification by faith') was problematic on two counts. First, it appeared to preserve the death of Jesus and 'the forgiveness of sins' as something exclusively concerned with the personal salvation of the individual rather than addressing the wider issues of evil and injustice within the world. Second, even within this personal context, it provided a less than integrated model for connecting this forgiveness to the transforming work of the Holy Spirit in our lives. Detached from the primary model being used to explain how our forgiveness was achieved, the importance of change taking place in our lives seemed to assume a less than central status.

In most presentations of penal substitution the emphasis is upon the wrath of God needing to be 'satisfied' through the death of Jesus, and this posed a similar difficulty. The problem was that it appeared to make the atonement less about changing either us or the reality of evil in the world and more to do with bringing about the resolution of conflicting attributes within God so that he could look on individuals differently. It thus became clear to me that a 'model' of the atonement was needed that would preserve all the strengths of 'penal substitution' while making certain adjustments that would address these areas of weakness. The strength of reaction against any suggestion of this, however, and the fact that it largely came from very affluent conservative evangelicals, reinforced my suspicion that this doctrine was possibly being cherished for the wrong reasons.

Evangelical attitudes towards biblical scholarship and treatment of the Bible itself

A related area of concern in my twenties was a broader one about the manner in which the evangelical tradition was apt to relate to both biblical scholarship and the Bible itself. As a history teacher, I was naturally drawn to gaining a clearer grasp of the historical background behind the events and theology presented in the Bible. This also felt inherently right, given the regular evangelical emphasis on our faith resting upon solid historical events rather than a set of abstract ideas. Despite this emphasis, however, it soon became clear to me that the evangelical tradition did not, for the most part, encourage the approach that historians are summoned to: revisiting the sources, looking for as much evidence as possible and being prepared, in the light of this, to consider fresh paradigms for understanding this data. People were aware that approaching the Gospels like this had in the past produced sceptical results, and naturally preferred to reassert, rather than re-examine, 'the deposit' of doctrine passed on to us. This was sometimes reinforced by the statement that since Jesus was alive, 'knowing him in *the present*' was what mattered most anyway. Historical research was broadly welcomed if it provided support for doctrine already established, but presented as rather unhelpful if it resulted in this doctrine being questioned. What disturbed me here was the lack of confidence in the historicity of the Bible's events that was exposed by this denial of the importance of investigation and enquiry. Something similar was evident at a more theological level, where the raising and acknowledgement of really searching questions about orthodoxy was generally presented as something rather 'untrusting' and destructive, rather than an important part of our stewardship of this doctrine.

These ideas often seemed to be coupled with the fact that evangelicalism, despite its official position, appeared to accord a rather secondary status to certain parts of Scripture. I began to appreciate the preponderance of narrative or story within both the Old and the New Testament, and became increasingly aware that the 'keys' for interpreting this narrative were overwhelmingly drawn from Reformation doctrine built upon a certain reading of Paul's epistles. Rather than being read and preached *as a story*, the Old Testament was more commonly used as a 'book of illustrations', with the consequent downplaying or even complete neglect of material less suited to this use. After a time I realized that this was equally true of the Gospels with sermons using much of their material to illustrate the truth of doctrinal points established from elsewhere. Sustained themes in the Gospels were therefore being neglected, the most obvious examples being their focus upon Jesus' inauguration of the kingdom of God/heaven, his confrontation with the powers of evil (through his exorcisms, healings and controversies) and his announcement of the type of judgement found in Matthew 23—25 (and its parallels in Mark 13 and Luke 21). In all three of these examples, a model of understanding based upon truths drawn from an interpretation of the Pauline epistles appeared to be neutralizing the most important emphases that large sections of the Gospels wanted to make. The sense of missing out on the intention behind the material, particularly within the Synoptic Gospels, resulted in me starting to search for a model of authority that would allow a reading and use of this material more faithful to the form in which we had received it.

Evangelical ambivalence towards 'the good things of creation'

Another area of weakness within the evangelical tradition, that took me rather longer to recognize, was its continuing ambivalence towards 'the good things of creation'. This was partly because it formed a more subtle version of a dualism that had previously been far more overt. Few within the evangelical subculture I grew up in were still following the strict instructions of previous generations of evangelicals to eschew things such as the theatre, cinema, make-up and alcohol. Much of the credit for provoking this loosening was given, within the folklore on which I was raised, to the influence of two evangelicals from overseas. One was the New Zealander Ted Schroeder, who as John Stott's curate in the 1960s persuaded him to take a more positive view of the theatre and cinema.[9] The other was the American Ruth Bell Graham, whose example as she arrived in the UK alongside husband Billy in 1954 was credited with leading many evangelical parents to relax their stance on make-up! Sport, which in any case had always occupied a somewhat more cherished place within the evangelical tradition, developed an even stronger endorsement through the emergence of organizations like Christians in Sport.[10] Thus within the youth groups, church house-parties and especially the Christian summer camps I attended as a teenager in the 1980s a very integrated model was presented, with drama, music and sport all playing a full and positive role within a Christian setting.

Uncertainty was apparent, however, at the level of a genuinely positive theology of creation to back up this integration and affirm the enjoyment of these parts of life outside of an explicitly Christian context. With hindsight, this was something that I needed particularly when, in my mid teens, I began to encounter a rich experience of life outside of church, from things such as music, drama and relationships. What I lacked from 'church' was theological input on why participation in these activities made me feel so alive. If I had pressed the question at the time, I imagine a measure of endorsement of these things might have been provoked, alongside a more assured caution about the danger of making such things of the world into idols and putting them before God. What wasn't apparent was much of a message concerning the God-given-ness of these 'good gifts of his creation', the challenge to enjoy them 'to the full' and an encouragement to the thoughtful and responsible stewardship of these gifts placed within a firmly positive context. Rather sadly, my teenage conclusion was that the major 'Christian issue' I faced was how to remain 'a believer' while not missing out on everything that life had to offer. This rather negative evaluation is, I believe, mirrored by that of many young people brought up in the church today. Looking back, I can see that a major part of its cause is that evangelicalism's strong doctrine of 'the fall' often fails to be balanced by an equally confident and thoughtfully applied doctrine of creation.

One result of this that I observed as I grew older was the increasing amount of secularism within evangelical subculture. Freed from the strong expectation of earlier generations that secular culture should be rejected, many adult as well as younger evangelicals were then exposed as being rather ill-equipped to evaluate the good and bad within this culture. Through the 1990s and 2000s the entertainment industry continued its expansion, with the proliferation of romantic comedies, reality TV shows and computer games, and it became clear to me that a far more sophisticated Christian model of engagement was needed to avoid the extreme alternatives of a complete rejection of secular culture or its uncritical acceptance. Older resources existed, such as Richard Niebuhr's *Christ and Culture*, to help this process; a number of newer books joined them in the 2000s, encouraging, for instance, theological reflection by Christians upon popular film.[11] What still appeared to be needed in popular evangelical consciousness, however, was a really strong theology of creation to make it clear why this sort of engagement was such a necessity.

A slightly different manifestation of this lack of integration was evangelicalism's frequent alienation of people who were particularly sensitive to art and beauty. Within the evangelical churches I belonged to, those who were artistic would often appear rather 'on the edge', seemingly because of the tradition's failure to endorse and reflect those things creating most resonance within them. Less true in general of music, this certainly went for other forms of artistic expression such as poetry, art and dance. The acknowledgement and encouragement of the expressive arts within the increasingly 'post-evangelical' atmosphere of the annual Greenbelt festival[12] once again pointed to the need for evangelicalism to be renewed by a deeper and far more meaningful doctrine of creation.

With hindsight, I can also see that this underdeveloped theology of creation was responsible for the ambivalence, or even distaste, with which some evangelicals in the 1980s viewed the emerging Green movement. Again, this reaction was very English in its nature, generally falling a long way short of the anti-Green polemic that emerged during the same period in the USA among more extreme evangelicals. At the root of this negative reaction, however, there appeared to be a similar fear that a strong concern for the care and preservation of the environment reflected pagan and pantheistic values rather than Christian ones. This attitude became less pronounced during the 1990s as concern for the environment became more mainstream and evangelicals generally became happier to espouse and, in some cases, strongly support a Green agenda. However, while God's instructions in Genesis to 'work' the Garden of Eden 'and take care of it' were cited to support this, how this stewardship of creation related to the Christian's more primary task of 'building up treasure in heaven' was left largely unexplained. As a result, most of the evangelicalism I encountered was still largely unsure about the extent to which it should be promoting a 'full on' Green agenda.

Evangelical ambivalence towards the sacraments

Another area of uncertainty that I observed 'growing up evangelical' was in regard to the sacraments. Once again, this uncertainty was subtle. An important aspect of the Keele Statement at the first National Evangelical Anglican Congress (NEAC1) in 1967 was its Article 76 expressing repentance at the failure of evangelicals 'to do justice to the Lord's Supper as the main service of the People of God'.[13] In the years that followed, particularly through the influence of Colin Buchanan upon Church of England liturgy, evangelical Anglicans increasingly recognized that they needed to place much greater importance upon sacramental worship.[14] One aspect of this change, occurring between the 1960s and 1980s, was the relocation of baptisms into the main service held on a Sunday in most evangelical Anglican churches.

The signs of a continuing evangelical ambivalence to the sacraments were nonetheless still apparent in that era. While many evangelicals I encountered could talk with a fair amount of ease about the danger of ritualism and expecting automatic blessing from the sacraments, there was much less confidence when it came to giving a really positive explanation of their value. Such explanations, when they were offered, were often little more than presenting the sacraments as a powerful visual aid, with a nod towards their 'mystery', allowing the discussion to stop there. A variation on this, witnessed more often in non-conformist evangelical circles, was to explain that the sacraments were important because they were 'a command' of Jesus. While outwardly affirming their significance, this appeared to declare that the sacraments should be treated with importance even though their provision made little real or rational sense.

As a result of all this I was left fairly unsure, after my confirmation in 1984, how to approach and appreciate Holy Communion. Sensing rather than understanding the need to regard Communion as an encounter with the risen Jesus rather than a bare memorial, I too settled upon seeing sacramental worship as something that I wasn't meant to understand. The problem then was that Holy Communion assumed a position of importance in my worship that was far below other things I could more easily understand, such as the value of sung worship, prayer, reading the Bible and listening to sermons. In later years I discovered that this was broadly true for most evangelical Christians. It was probably this factor, exacerbated rather than created by the growth of 'family' and 'seeker-friendly' services, that resulted in evangelicals in the Church of England failing to fulfil the Keele commitment 'to work towards the practice of a weekly celebration of the sacrament as the central corporate service of the church'.[15] I observed the depth of spiritual refreshment and renewal that Anglo-Catholics received from 'the Eucharist', and also the way in which, at their best, they were able to integrate this sacramental worship into other areas of their spiritual lives and mission.[16] This made me keen to locate a biblical theology that could bring about something similar for evangelicals.

Evangelical ambivalence towards the Church

A final area of uncertainty that I detected among evangelicals was in regard to their ecclesiology, or theology of church. Once again I was aware of progress, since evangelicals within the Church of England had moved a long way beyond the 'best boat to fish from' and ghetto mentality of the 1950s, towards a far more positive attitude towards the Church of which they were part. Keele had been a crucial staging post here too, with its theme of 'Involvement' signalling a decisive commitment by evangelicals to 'get stuck in' to the Church of England. My father was very much a 'Keele evangelical', later becoming an Archdeacon and then the Church of England's Director of Ministry, so this mentality of 'involvement' in the wider Church was one that was deeply impressed upon me as I grew up.

Whether the resolve shown at Keele then translated itself into a proper evangelical ecclesiology is debatable. Robert Runcie, when he was Archbishop of Canterbury, obviously thought not, speaking at the third National Evangelical Anglican 'Celebration' at Caister in 1988 of evangelicals' lack of 'any noticeable ecclesiological thinking' and issuing a call to evangelicals in the Church of England to give 'more explicit attention to the doctrine of the church'.[17] This challenge was accepted as valid by some, while others said that Runcie simply didn't like the ecclesiology that evangelicals possessed.[18] What was certainly clear to me through that era, however, was that for the majority of evangelicals I encountered, 'church' was essentially the local group of people with whom *they chose* to worship God in order to be spiritually fed and serve him effectively. The teaching to place the greatest value upon a personal relationship with God led to a tendency for this 'personal relationship' to become *an individual one* and when combined with an increasingly 'consumer' mentality this could result in a very 'functional' ecclesiology. The acceptance of 'shopping around to find the right church' and prioritizing reasons for attendance by what was helpful to one's personal 'growth' were both fairly obvious indicators of this; although this was just as frequently offset by a rich sense of community and the earnest desire to be God's people serving him in the local area.

Overall, therefore, it would probably be fair to say that any 'theology of church' that I observed among most evangelical Anglicans I worshipped alongside was not particularly different from that I encountered within independent churches. Exceptions existed, of course; a small number of lay people showed a keen interest in the wider Church of England, particularly its synods and committees, and occasionally made outstanding contributions there. But on the whole, particularly as so many people in evangelical Anglican churches come from other denominations, any broader understanding of 'church' tended to be rather vague and undefined. The weakness in this theology of church was most apparent when it came to relating to other Christians whose beliefs and practices were significantly different from those of evangelicals. Here, while positive noises were made from time to time about the importance of 'church unity', there was rarely any specific and practical teaching as to how we, as evangelicals, could meaningfully exist in the same church with those from other traditions. With the lack of instruction on this issue, it became much easier for something of an evangelical superiority complex over 'non-Bible-believing' Christians to develop. The worst forms of this could be challenged with, for example, 'Do not judge or you too will be judged' (Matthew 7.1), but I was still left searching for a theology of church that could be generous and inclusive without being unprincipled and unconcerned about truth.

Issues awaiting an answer . . .

My reason for sharing these elements of my personal story is that I believe that the issues I have raised have a much wider relevance. Within the UK at least, a growing theological uncertainty seems to have played a significant role in creating something of a crisis of confidence in contemporary evangelicalism.[19] The growth of a postmodern uncertainty about 'doctrine' has contributed to this. The nature of the Greenbelt festival, however, and other manifestations of 'post-evangelicalism', indicate that many who still value something of the *spirituality* of evangelicalism are now inclined to doubt whether the evangelical tradition contains the answers to the world's big problems. Nowhere is this truer than among those concerned for holistic mission. Here there is an increasing sense that 'middle-class evangelicalism' is probably more connected to the problem of injustice than to its solution. Protests against the triteness of evangelical doctrine and practice in the UK from leaders such as Steve Chalke and others have their source in this frustration.[20] Concern about the strong influence of evangelicalism upon perceived American imperialism, especially in the wake of the war in Iraq, has also played an important role. Establishing that biblical orthodoxy is radical and truly 'good news for the poor', rather than being oriented towards the status quo, is therefore vital both to keeping these important groupings within the evangelical tradition and to seeing its overall renewal.

In the light of these issues, the unwillingness or inability to engage with Tom Wright's theology reported in Chapter 1 is shown to be a major problem. The summary of Wright's thought that follows in the next chapter is written to encourage more of this engagement and, in particular, further understanding of the compelling answers that Wright has provided to the issues covered within this chapter. It is my opinion that, as well as providing a convincing response to these issues, Wright's theology will be found to address a number of others as well, some of which are touched upon in the later chapters of this book.

3

A summary of the theology of
N. T. Wright

It seems to be that the longer people have been Christians, the trickier it can be for them to 'get it' in relation to Tom Wright's theology. This is not because Wright has a difficult writing style. Compared to most theologians and biblical commentators, the very opposite is true: his style has even been described 'as smooth as fine chocolate'![1] He has also shown a great commitment to communicating on a popular level as well as the academic. The reason, as indicated in Chapter 1, lies largely with the difficulty that some Christians have of stepping out of one paradigm or 'interpretative framework' and into another. This is particularly the case when familiar words, concepts and passages from the Bible are used in a rather different manner from that which people are used to hearing. If a bridge into this new understanding is lacking, such a message is often simply 'not heard'. I include myself here, as one who had been reading Wright's books for some time before the 'penny dropped' and I was able to recognize the distinctive understanding that he was proposing.

What follows is an attempt to present, as clearly as possible, the key 'building blocks' that make up that overall paradigm proposed by Tom Wright for understanding the New Testament. These are grouped under key words (or phrases) in order to enable the reader to establish 'pegs' on which to hang the rest of Wright's thinking. This description is not exhaustive, deliberately so in the hope of meeting its aim of providing a simple and 'graspable' introduction to his thought.[2]

History

First of all, Wright is unashamedly historical in his approach to understanding Jesus and the New Testament. Such study is neither needlessly complex nor only for those who are 'into that sort of thing' and want to fill out their understanding of some of its details. It is illegitimate to claim that laying too much importance upon contingent history will detract from Jesus' 'timeless' significance, or that since Jesus is alive 'knowing him now' makes such study unnecessary.[3] The root of all of these attempts to avoid engagement with history, Wright suggests, has usually been a fear of what might be discovered about Jesus if such study is carried through.[4]

In response, Wright argues that the Enlightenment's legacy of separating history from faith must be firmly rejected, since a proper understanding of the significance of Jesus is possible only through serious study of him within his historical context.[5] Without such historical enquiry, Wright argues, there is no proper check on our human propensity to remake Jesus and therefore Christianity into whatever form we wish them to take.[6] Warnings from relatively recent history indicate the dangers of this, and were indeed responsible for the renewal of the 'quest for the historical Jesus' from the early 1950s.[7] More positively, such historical enquiry and the calling of Christianity back to its historical roots is the only path to the full relevance and exciting challenge of Jesus for today being discovered.[8]

Critical realism

In his approach to studying 'the historical Jesus', Wright rejects the method of the 'Jesus seminar', with its supposed 'objective criteria' for establishing which 'Jesus sayings' within the Gospels are authentic and which were 'composed' by the early church.[9] Wright argues that the correct method for studying Jesus should be similar to that taken with other ancient historical characters such as Alexander the Great and Julius Caesar.[10] This approach, which he describes as 'critical realism', seeks to establish a hypothesis about Jesus that will do three things: include all the data that we have about him without distortion, possess an essential simplicity or consistency of line, and have the ability to shed light on other related questions.[11] In the case of this third point, Wright argues that any reconstruction of Jesus has to be credible (even if deeply subversive) both within the context of first-century Judaism, and as *the starting point* for (rather than being identical to) the beliefs Christians held about Jesus by the early second century.[12] Wright particularly argues that an understanding of Jesus must be found that will make sense of the fact that within a very short space of time he was being worshipped by Jewish Christians who were still insistently monotheistic.[13]

Story

Central to Wright's approach in establishing the setting of Jesus within first-century Judaism is the importance that he gives to the category of 'story'.[14] He argues that all societies construct their 'world-views' within explicit or implicit narratives, and shows how these 'controlling stories' go on to shape the way in which people live (their 'habitual praxis'), the fundamental symbols they create or use around this, and the answers that they give to key questions.[15] From this basis, it is possible to establish the 'mindset' of individuals from making sense of their actions against the overall narrative context in which they are set.[16]

The story of Israel

An acknowledgement of all these factors necessitates paying full attention to the story of Israel as we seek to understand Jesus.[17] Rather than being interpreted as free-standing narratives that happen to have some resonances with earlier traditions, the Gospels present Jesus as the climactic act within a play that the Israelites had been acting for centuries (see Matthew 1.1–17). Other early Christian writings possess much the same emphasis (see Paul's reference to 'our fathers' in 1 Corinthians 10.1). Wright is clear that acknowledging the story of Israel is very definitely not the same as identifying certain parts of the Old Testament that can be seen as prophecies about Jesus, or 'types' foreshadowing his work.[18] Paying proper attention to the story of Israel is instead about recognizing the overall 'controlling narrative' that shaped the Jewish world-view within which Jesus lived and which produced its resulting praxis and symbols. This narrative is largely what we know as the Old Testament, which presents itself as a continuous story. Engaging with the nature, shape and direction of this story, including its search for an 'ending', is therefore crucial to understanding the place of Jesus within it and the Gospels' understanding of his overall significance.[19]

Covenant

Central to the story of the Old Testament and the whole driver for biblical theology is God's calling of Abraham to undo the sin of Adam and its effect on the world. The 'covenant' that God made with Abraham, therefore, and his election of Israel, was made precisely *in order* to carry forward his plan for undoing the effect of evil and restoring his creation.[20] The promise to Abraham of a land was the start of God's plan for reclaiming and renewing the entire world. The promise to Abraham of a family was likewise the start of God's plan for populating this restored world with a worldwide family. It is from this concrete basis that the rest of the Bible's holistic approach to salvation proceeds, and also the continuity between the Old and New Testament. Rather than God's people living in God's land being an inadequate earthly prototype for a later 'more spiritual' understanding of salvation, the covenant with Israel indicates the start of God's plan for a renewed earth ruled over by his renewed people.[21]

Monotheism

Indicated not just in Genesis but especially in Isaiah and the Psalms, this interrelationship of creation and covenant is the key factor in understanding the nature of Jewish monotheism (its belief in the oneness of God). Monotheism was not primarily generated by concern about the proper numerical analysis of the inner being of God; it was driven by belief in one creator God that enabled Israel to avoid both idolatry (making created things into gods) and 'dualism' (denying the goodness of God's creation because of the evil afflicting it).[22] From this basis, Wright uses the terms 'creational/covenantal monotheism' to describe Judaism's belief in the commitment of the one God, YHWH (his special covenant name), to take the action needed to restore his creation through his chosen people.[23]

Righteousness, Torah and Temple

A central feature of Wright's thought is his understanding of 'the righteousness of God' as the key term used in the Old Testament to speak of God's commitment to this covenant plan to rescue and renew his creation.[24] Wright stresses the role within this plan of the law, or Torah, as a 'covenant charter' that promised life to Israel through its call to live as fully human beings. It was also intended to offer hope to the surrounding world through its witness of how God's 'image-bearing' creatures could fulfil his creation mandate by ruling faithfully over that creation. Rather than being understood as the means by which Israel earned God's righteousness, the law was seen as the way of life for the people God had saved through his dramatic actions at Passover and the crossing of the Red Sea.[25] The Tabernacle and later the Temple also play an important role in the overall covenant plan by establishing YHWH's presence in the land among his covenant people. They acted as a foretaste of his intention to flood the whole world one day with his presence (see Isaiah 11.9).[26]

The story of the covenant people in the Old Testament takes many twists and turns, not least the way in which Israel herself fails to keep the law, to avoid sin and thus to embrace her calling to be a light to the Gentiles.[27] Rather than remaining distinct from the pagans, Israel's tendency is to become 'like the nations', which ironically results in constant oppression at their hands. Throughout, however, God's righteousness is maintained as he works alongside and sometimes through Israel's failures to rescue them and keep his covenant plan alive. Wright lays a particular emphasis here upon God's commitment to continue working through the ambiguities that are present in Israel's response to him.[28] An example of this is Israel's desire for a monarchy, which results in the incorporation of God's promise to David within the covenant plan. Israel continued to sin, however, and eventually the Temple was destroyed by her enemies, and the people taken from the land and into exile in Babylon (2 Kings 25).[29] The exile served as a symbol of Israel's recapitulation of the sin of Adam and Eve, corresponding to their expulsion from Eden after their disobedience. At this point of exile, with the covenant tested to the limit, the Psalms go back to creation in their appeal to God to fulfil his 'righteousness' (Psalm 74, for example).[30] Similarly, Isaiah 40—55, with the additional message that the path to covenant renewal will somehow come through the suffering of God's 'servant'. The book of Daniel also reflects this theme, indicating Israel's eventual vindication after suffering at the hands of pagans.[31]

Exile

This is one of Wright's most distinctive themes, emphasizing the assumption of most first-century Jews that Israel was still in a state of exile.[32] Daniel 9 is an important text here, reflection upon its reference to the exile lasting 70 times 7 years being evident within several strands of first-century Judaism. While the Jewish people had returned from *geographical* exile in Babylon in 539 BC, their belief in a continuing state of exile was caused by the continued oppression of Israel by evil, chiefly in the form of foreign, pagan rule. The promises of a restoration after exile contained in Deuteronomy, Isaiah 40—55, Daniel, Ezekiel and other parts of the Old Testament had spoken of a complete liberation, with an emphasis on 'a greater exodus' and YHWH returning to Zion (Jerusalem) to 'become king' in a decisively new way.[33] Wright argues that since no one could claim that these events had occurred, these dramatic promises were still seen by the majority of first-century Jews as awaiting fulfilment. The common expectation was that this would involve their Gentile oppressors being put in their place and the Temple properly restored.[34] Against this context, the phrase 'forgiveness of sins' was most naturally understood to refer to the liberation of Israel as a whole from exile, as God acted to fulfil covenant promises. This leads to Wright's assertion that first-century Jews were very aware that they were living within 'a story in search of an ending'.[35]

Eschatology

This leads to a particularly important point. The key issue for Jews in the first century was not, 'what will happen to me when I die?' (they believed that they would somehow be safe in God) but, 'when will YHWH bring about the liberation of Israel?'[36] The crucial issue was one of eschatology but with this concept needing to be freed from the widespread misconception that the Jews understood this climax to their history to mean the end or destruction of the world.[37]

Emphasizing the very Jewish understanding of the original goodness of God's creation, Wright argues that Jewish eschatological expectation was therefore concerned with the earth's *transformation* and *renewal* by a fresh act of God.[38] The creational and covenantal monotheism at the heart of Judaism ensured that this was the very opposite of any dualistic belief in the irredeemable nature of the present physical world and its eventual destruction. A vital part of this is Wright's explanation of the nature of Jewish apocalyptic language which, he argues, is completely misunderstood by both fundamentalists and many critical biblical scholars when it is read as referring to a 'cosmic meltdown'. Wright argues that in a first-century context such language would have been clearly identified as metaphor, used in order to invest concrete earthly events with their full cosmic significance.[39]

Wright also points to the emergence of the term 'gospel' or 'good news' to describe the end of Israel's exile and this expected liberation of creation.[40] The idea of a 'messiah' acting as an agent of God to bring this about was a further development from this context.[41] The hope of Israel was not, therefore, for any sort of post-mortem disembodied bliss, but a national liberation that would fulfil the expectations created by the regular remembrance of the Exodus and raised by more recent events, particularly the Maccabean victory over their Syrian oppressors in the second century BC.

Those benefiting from the status quo, such as the Sadducees and Herodians, had no time for such eschatology, which completely challenged their quietist political agenda. The Essenes, 'Zealot' groups, and Pharisees, on the other hand, had clear (if significantly different) eschatological visions, all seeing God acting to restore his creation and vindicate his true people.[42]

A note of ambiguity in this eschatological vision existed with regard to the Gentiles.[43] The original calling of Abraham had spoken of 'all peoples' being blessed through him, and a number of passages in the Old Testament continued to assert that when YHWH returned to Zion, the Gentiles would also be caught up in his worship (for example, Isaiah 2.1–5; 19.18–25). Just as important to Israel's future hope, however, was the belief that her exile would be ended by YHWH decisively defeating Israel's enemies through his messianic agent. The destruction of the successive powers that had oppressed them and the consequent vindication of faithful Israel in the vision in Daniel 7 particularly resonated with many Jews as their oppression continued at the hands of Rome. Against this context, most first-century Jews therefore imagined that when YHWH acted to end the exile and defeat their enemies, this would largely involve the destruction of those Gentiles who were oppressing them.

Heaven

Within this context, Wright stresses the importance of appreciating the integrated cosmology (understanding of the nature of the universe) presented in the Old Testament. Central to this is an understanding of 'heaven' and 'earth' as the two interlocking spheres of God's single creation.[44] 'Earth' forms the world of space, time and matter within this created order that we most obviously experience, with 'heaven' understood as that dimension where the spiritual realities in God's creation are most obviously present. Normally hidden from human sight, 'heaven' was occasionally unveiled to the Old Testament prophets (see 2 Kings 6.17; Isaiah 6).[45] This allowed these prophets to both see and speak of the spiritual realities lying behind the 'earthly' events happening within Israel's history. They were also able to speak of God's ultimate intention to restore his creation by re-joining a renewed heaven with a renewed earth (Isaiah 65—66).[46]

Resurrection

The hope of resurrection belongs completely within this framework of creation, covenant and eschatology. Rather than being part of people's private spirituality, resurrection was a deeply radical doctrine, carrying with it all the associations of Israel's return from exile and their restoration as God's renewed people within his renewed creation.[47] Charting its development, Wright shows how the idea of resurrection was first used as a metaphor for the nation of Israel's future vindication when they were released from exile (see Ezekiel 37). Without losing this meaning, from around the third century BC resurrection developed a more literal sense as well, referring to God's raising of the dead to receive vindication or judgement (Daniel 12.1–3). From this basis, the concept of resurrection became the ultimate sign of God's commitment, not only to vindicate his people, but to restore his creation.[48]

Wright is keen to emphasize the politically subversive nature of belief in resurrection. Particularly developed during the Maccabean period of Syrian oppression, resurrection was subversive because if death was one day to be defeated, the tyrant knew he had no weapons left.[49] Physical resurrection (and anything else, Wright says, is not resurrection) of the true People of God therefore lay at the heart of

Pharisaic theology and that of most first-century Jewish groups looking for God's coming liberation to provide 'the right ending' to the story in which they were living. Belief in such a resurrection was completely rejected, on the other hand, by the wealthy and aristocratic Sadducees, chiefly because of their desire to preserve the political status quo.[50]

Praxis and symbols

It was this eschatology that shaped the praxis (or practice) by which Jewish people lived and the symbols that were crucial to them.[51] For groups such as the Pharisees the crucial praxis, as dictated in the present by this eschatology, was Israel maintaining its God-given distinctiveness over and against the pagan nations. Keeping Torah, most principally its distinctive symbols of circumcision, food laws and Sabbath observance, was understood by Jews in the diaspora (outside of Israel) as the *present* 'markers' of those whom God would vindicate (or in the covenant language employed by some of the Psalms, 'justify' or 'declare righteous') when he finally acted to fulfil his promises. The 'markers' for those in 'the land' were the land itself, Jerusalem and the Temple, with the food laws, Sabbath and circumcision all clustered around. Wright, like other recent scholars who assert this, rejects any idea that Judaism was a system of self-salvation. Rather than referring to deeds done to earn God's salvation, the phrase 'works of the law' indicated those prized badges of identity that were understood as marking out the true members of the people of God who could one day expect to be restored by him.[52]

Prophet

Against this historical context, Wright argues that the best *initial* model with which to understand Jesus is that of a prophet whose words and actions were part of delivering an urgent eschatological message to Israel.[53] In justifying this, Wright points to the number of indications within the Gospels that Jesus modelled his ministry on that of Old Testament prophets sent to Israel by their covenant God to warn them of the imminent consequences of the direction in which they were heading and summoning them to a new and different way.[54] Within this, and in a manner similar to John the

Baptist, Jesus combined the model of an 'oracular prophet', bringing his message through spoken words and symbolic actions, and a 'leadership prophet', leading a renewal movement for the reconstitution of Israel.[55]

Kingdom

Specifically, Jesus of Nazareth proclaimed that through him God was bringing the coming of his kingdom, or rule, to Israel and the world. The stories Jesus told, the signs he performed, the praxis he encouraged and the attitude he showed towards the established symbols of Judaism all demonstrated that, through his ministry, God was bringing the exile to an end and ushering in his new eschatological age.[56] Signs such as Jesus' multiplication of loaves and fishes and turning water into wine were intended to symbolize the covenant renewal of Israel that he was bringing. Other signs, such as the calming of the storm, revealed Jesus' power over the natural order and indicated how this covenant renewal was going to lead to the ultimate restoration of the whole of creation.[57]

A number of Jesus' actions showed his belief that with the coming of the kingdom it was now time for Israel to let go of those parts of the Jewish law that were given to keep her separate from the rest of the world. Rather than being bad in themselves, these symbols were no longer necessary because the exile had ended. Jesus' healings in particular indicated the bestowing of 'shalom' or eschatological peace, not just through their provision of physical health for those healed but their reintegration into the people of YHWH. The strict enforcement of boundaries was therefore replaced by welcome and open table fellowship as the praxis and symbols of the new kingdom, with sinners especially welcomed by Jesus to demonstrate the great act of restoration now taking place.[58] Symbols of ethnic separation, such as Sabbath observance, food laws and family identity, were also now relativized, as the arrival of the kingdom meant that the need for such defensiveness should give way to the renewal of Israel's vocation to be a light to the world.[59] While Jesus' ministry was largely focused upon Israel (Matthew 10.5–6; 15.24), some of his words and actions showed his awareness that this process would eventually lead to the incorporation of Gentiles into the people of God as well (Matthew 8.5–13).[60]

It was these actions that account for the fierce opposition that Jesus received from groups such as the Pharisees, for whom the symbols and praxis being discarded went to the heart of their entire world-view. Wright rejects as anachronistic any understanding of the conflict between the Pharisees and Jesus being one of legalism or 'outward observance' against 'inward spirituality'. The conflict was instead about alternative political agendas generated by alternative eschatological beliefs, with both the actions and non-actions that Jesus promoted being seen by the Pharisees as undermining anti-pagan zeal and leading Israel badly astray.[61]

While Wright does at some points use the word 'inclusion' to describe the welcome 'for everyone' into the kingdom that Jesus issued, he is careful to avoid any sense that this came without challenge. He sums this up through the phrase, 'Jesus . . . met people where they were but didn't leave them there,' emphasizing that when Jesus 'included' people and incorporated them into the community, they were also transformed both physically and morally, indicating the eschatological nature of the kingdom he was announcing.[62]

Repentance

Repentance was reflected in much of Jesus' teaching as he issued a challenge to Israel to recognize the coming of God's kingdom and follow him into a new way of living that demonstrated its reality. As part of this, Wright argues for a much broader understanding of 'repentance' than the term is often given. Rather than simply referring to an individual's acceptance of a state of personal sin and contrition about this, Jesus' call to repentance was far more historically specific. Emphasizing a similar use of the term by Josephus as he addressed Jewish rebels, Wright understands Jesus' call to repentance as a challenge to Israel to exchange its path towards revolution against Rome for a very different approach.[63]

The Sermon on the Mount, rather than being generalized ethical teaching, belongs within this context and represents the challenge of Jesus to Israel to be renewed in its vocation and live as the new covenant people of God.[64] Certain parts of it, such as the challenge to be 'a city on a hill' and not a 'house built on sand', are quite specific in their reference to Jerusalem and the Temple. In deliberate contrast to the alternative agendas on offer at that time, the vocation that

Jesus proclaimed to Israel involved the refusal to repay evil with evil and the willingness to suffer as the path by which God's light would come to the world and his people receive their vindication.[65] Israel had been reconstituted through 'the forgiveness of sins'; showing a similar forgiveness to both Israel's enemies and one another was presented by Jesus as a crucial indication of entry into the kingdom (Matthew 18.21–35).[66] Central to this renewal of the covenant was a necessary renewal of the heart, as Jesus called Israel back to God's original intention in creation, before the law was provided for 'the hardness of hearts' (see Mark 10.1–12).[67]

Through his symbolic gathering of twelve disciples (recalling the original twelve tribes of Israel) Jesus demonstrated that he was reconstituting the people of God around himself and summoning her to this radical kingdom agenda.[68] These actions, together with the summons that Jesus made to faith in him, and his willingness to grant forgiveness of sins outside of the official structures, were further indications that allegiance to the symbols of Torah and Temple should be replaced with allegiance to him.[69]

Evil

In the course of this activity, Jesus was clear that he was launching the decisive battle with Israel's enemies. Rather than simply identifying these with Israel's pagan oppressors and her renegade leaders, Jesus saw the real enemy as Satan/Beelzebub and the cosmic powers of evil and darkness.[70] This accounts for the prominence of the exorcisms that Jesus performed (see Mark 1.21–28), his statements about Beelzebub (Mark 3.20–30) and his emphasis upon a necessary renewal of the heart for Israel herself (Mark 7.1–23). It also accounts for Jesus' refusal to make common ground with a Jewish resistance movement seeking to use evil's weapons in their efforts to defeat that same evil.[71] This, according to Wright, is the context against which to understand the temptations that Jesus faced just before the start of his prophetic career, where he refused to compromise with Satan (Matthew 4.1–11).[72] His statements about his followers not seeking power (Mark 10.35–45) or using violence to further the coming of the kingdom of God (Luke 9.51–56; Matthew 26.47–56; John 18.36f.) also reflect his understanding of the real enemies that Israel faced. Instead, Jesus promoted a very different way in which a willingness to suffer and let evil do its worst would bring about both vindication for his followers and 'the victory of God'.[73]

Parables

The underlying mode of much of Jesus' ministry was therefore a retelling of the story of Israel through words and deeds in a manner that pointed to its unexpected fulfilment. Central to this was Jesus' use of parables, with their 'secret' nature having parallels to the subversive nature of Jewish apocalyptic literature.[74] Jesus' telling of these parables was in itself a means by which he saw the kingdom coming, with its 'mysteries' being revealed to those 'with ears to hear', while remaining incomprehensible to those failing to recognize its arrival. Wright describes this struggle of Jesus' hearers to understand his parables as 'the struggle for a new world to be born'.[75] The parables told during Jesus' Galilean ministry, such as The Sower and The Prodigal Son, were far from being simple teaching about general spiritual truths; in reality they were specific and indeed sophisticated stories concerning the return of Israel from exile and the need to recognize that this was happening but not in the way that people had expected.[76]

Other parables Jesus told once he arrived in Jerusalem spoke in a similarly 'hidden' manner of the coming of the kingdom of God. Here Wright rejects the common assumption that in parables such as The Talents and The Ten Bridesmaids, Jesus was giving 'long-distance teaching' about his 'second coming'. These parables were again very specific messages concerning the return of YHWH to Zion at that moment in time, and the serious consequences of Israel's failure to recognize this.[77] Retelling a storyline in which judgement was normally associated with YHWH acting against the pagan nations, the surprising element in the parables was that judgement would actually be for those Jews missing YHWH's return.

The fall of Jerusalem

Wright argues that, as with the Old Testament prophets, Jesus' warnings about judgement had a very concrete reference. If Israel missed the fact that God's kingdom was arriving, and continued to follow her alternative agendas, rather than the one that Jesus was announcing, the result would be the destruction of Jerusalem and its Temple at the hands of Rome.[78] This was not an arbitrary threat; this punishment would simply be the consequence of the path that Israel had chosen to follow. This accounts for the prophetic act of judgement that Jesus performed when he overturned the tables of the money-changers in the Temple and, in particular, his accusation about it having become 'a den of brigands'.[79]

Once again, Wright's claim is that passages frequently understood as being about Jesus' second coming, 'the rapture' and 'the end of the world' have been badly misread, chiefly through a failure to appreciate the nature of apocalyptic language. Such language, he argues, with its statements about 'the sun being darkened' and 'stars falling from the sky', was commonly understood Jewish metaphor of the time, used to speak of the cosmic significance of actual historical events.[80] A modern equivalent of this would be speaking of the fall of the Berlin Wall in 1989 as 'an earth-shattering event'.[81] The passages in Mark 13 (and its parallels in Matthew 24 and Luke 21) use this heavily symbolic language, therefore, to refer to the fall of Jerusalem and the destruction of the Temple.[82]

Jesus' reference to Daniel 7, with its image of the Son of Man 'coming on the clouds', is particularly important here. Rather than using this image to speak of his future *descent* to earth, Jesus instead used its original meaning in Daniel to speak symbolically of the vindication that God's true humanity would receive when his prophetic judgement upon Israel was fulfilled through the Temple's desecration and destruction by the pagan powers in AD 70.[83] This accounts for the statements Jesus made about some of his followers not tasting death until they saw the kingdom coming in power (Mark 9.1), and also the practical instructions to his followers on how to escape being caught up in this judgement (Mark 13.14–23). The resurrection and Ascension of Jesus also fulfil these predictions, in tandem with the destruction of the Temple, and all form part of the Gospels' story of how Jesus became God's appointed king over the world.

Messiah/Christ

For Wright it is very clear that Jesus' words and actions demonstrated a clear self-understanding of his messianic role in bringing about Israel's return from exile, the defeat of evil and return of YHWH to Zion. He firmly rejects attempts to deny such intentionality to Jesus, and argues that his messianic self-understanding is shown by the nature of his entry into Jerusalem, the Davidic claims made within the 'royal riddles' he spoke there (Mark 12.1–17, 35–40), the 'anointing' that he permitted to occur at Bethany (Mark 14.1–11) and the authority he claimed through his action in the Temple.[84] All of these built upon the nature of Jesus' actions during his earlier prophetic ministry, such as his invoking of the example of David to express his authority over the Sabbath (Mark 2.24–28).[85]

From this basis, Jesus understood his role as Messiah to act as Israel's representative by fulfilling her calling to become a servant and endure suffering and death as the means of gaining her deliverance.[86] Wright argues for the strong plausibility of Jesus having this mindset, given the manner in which previous prophets such as Ezekiel had symbolically undergone the fate they announced would happen to Jerusalem as a whole.[87] He also points to how an understanding of redemptive suffering through the 'messianic woes' had developed from the Maccabean period onwards.[88] Understanding that Israel's failure to be a light to the world had led her to imminent judgement, Jesus, as Israel's Messiah, then chose to share in that fate by taking the path of obedient servanthood that led to his death on the cross. The actions he took during the Last Supper suggest that Jesus recognized his death to be accomplishing the real exodus and the two most commonly understood tasks of the Messiah: rebuilding the Temple and defeating Israel's enemies.[89] The latter would happen by Jesus allowing evil to do its worst, meaning that its power would be spent and only remain upon those who had excluded themselves from the renewed Israel that Jesus had reconstituted.

Atonement in the Gospels

Rejecting the idea that the Gospels contain little atonement theology, Wright shows the extent to which their narratives are constructed around the theme of how God had dealt with sin and evil.[90] The Gospels depict the full extent of this evil in the oppressive political powers of the day, the misguided agendas of Israel, the flawed nature of Jesus' own followers and the deep forces of darkness lying behind all this; they then describe the death of Jesus as resulting from all these forms of evil coming together. The way in which this evil is then dealt with follows on from the earlier parts of the Gospel narratives in which Jesus is shown as overcoming evil by completely engaging with those caught up in it, such as people with leprosy and tax collectors.[91] In his death, Jesus took this identification to the fullest extent possible, being obedient to the vocation that he had announced to Israel in the Sermon on the Mount, and taking on himself the direct consequences of her failure and sin. Building on the prophets' words of an approaching tribulation and warning his disciples to 'stay awake' to avoid it (Mark 14.38), Jesus is shown as carrying this evil so that, through being allowed to do its worst, its power could be exhausted and broken.[92] From the Gospel writers' point of view, it was because of Jesus' role as Israel's representative Messiah or King that his death enabled God's judgement to be executed upon sin, thus bringing Israel's exile finally to an end. Wright goes so far as to suggest that the Gospel writers are telling their whole story to explain why the resurrection of Jesus had happened. Rather than being a rather bizarre miracle, it was the appropriate result of cosmic and global evil being confronted with the saving love of Israel's covenant, creator God.[93]

Wright therefore emphasizes how the full story of Israel and the covenant, the nature of the Gospel narratives and the messianic meaning of 'Christ' are all indispensable for understanding 'the atonement'. Reducing the Old Testament's significance here to include some elements that simply foreshadow the atonement or act as illustrations or types for it, and seeing the Gospels as providing 'the description' for which the epistles supply 'the theology', is to miss much that is vital for really understanding the atonement.[94] He also emphasizes the nature of all 'theories of the atonement' as abstractions from the actual historical events that must remain primary for understanding the significance of Jesus' death.[95]

Jesus and God

Beyond understanding his ministry in prophetic and messianic terms, Wright is clear that Jesus recognized his actions to be not only proclaiming YHWH's return to Zion, but *embodying* this return.[96] Through the telling of stories about a king returning to Zion to judge and to save, Jesus' symbolic actions revealed that he was doing what, according to the Scriptures, YHWH alone had promised to do. This self-understanding, signalled by the nature of his entry into Jerusalem (Mark 11.1–11),[97] was also shown by the way in which Jesus presented himself as replacing the Temple, both during his earlier ministry and through the actions surrounding his death.[98] Jesus showed himself as the one in whom God was at last becoming present, and this reached its climax in his trial before Caiaphas (Mark 14. 53–64). His claim to share YHWH's throne in the manner spoken of in Daniel 7 led to the decision that he was guilty of blasphemy.[99]

Wright, however, resists concluding from this that Jesus 'knew he was God', in the sense of someone intellectually knowing a piece of information. Emphasizing the highest form of knowing to be that of relational love, Wright instead suggests that Jesus' knowledge of his divine identity was vocational. From his experience of struggling obedience, faith and prayer, Jesus understood himself to be called to do and be for Israel what only YHWH could do and be.[100] He believed this was true and acted decisively on this belief. It was the resurrection of Jesus which then convinced the early Christians that since God's purposes had been fulfilled through what he had done, Jesus should be worshipped.[101] Built upon the Jewish understanding of YHWH, this worship of Jesus was therefore understood as *expressing* rather than in any way compromising Israel's monotheism.[102]

The resurrection of Jesus

The resurrection of Jesus thus formed the decisive indication to the early Christians that the exile was indeed over and God's new eschatological age had dawned. The resurrection of Jesus was also what convinced them that the sole means of receiving this reality, and the Spirit that indicated its presence, was through Jesus as the one that had been vindicated as Israel's Messiah.[103] Wright argues against the Gospel accounts of Jesus' resurrection being constructed sometime later to 'embody' an originally more 'spiritual' understanding of what had happened at Easter. Their lack of 'theological development' instead gives a strong indication of their nature as carefully preserved primary accounts.[104]

The resurrection of Jesus was crucial for St Paul because, as a Pharisee, he already firmly believed in the resurrection as the sign of the coming of God's new age of vindication.[105] He realized, after his experience on the Damascus road, that what he expected to happen to all God's people at *the end* of the present age had now happened to the one man Jesus *in the middle* of it, indicating that God's eschatological age had broken into the world through him.[106] This moved Paul to recognize that Jesus was indeed the Messiah of Israel his followers were claiming him to be.[107]

Central to the focus of his future ministry as 'the apostle to the Gentiles' Paul was particularly aware that the resurrection had established Jesus not only as Israel's Messiah but, as a consequence, Lord of the whole world. This then meant that Jesus was the one whom *all* nations must now be summoned to obey.[108] Paul's understanding here was built upon the clarity with which the Old Testament spoke of Israel's Messiah also being Lord of the world (Psalms 2 and 72; Isaiah 9 and 11, for example). Rather than needing such Jewish categories to be transcended or abandoned for the 'universal' significance of Jesus to result, belief in Jesus as Israel's Messiah directly led to this.

Gospel

This is what Paul meant by 'the gospel' or 'good news'. According to Wright, the gospel does not refer to the means by which individuals can be 'saved' and 'go to heaven when they die'. It refers to the royal proclamation that in and through Jesus, declared by his resurrection to be Messiah and Lord, YHWH the God of Israel has become King and begun his process of putting his world right.[109] Wright shows how this understanding is completely consistent with the original use of the term 'good news' in Isaiah 40.9 and 52.7, with its implicit challenge to that term being used in a similar way by pagan emperors. An integral part of this gospel proclamation is that through the coming of God's Spirit everyone, without restriction, is summoned to be part of this renewed world that he is remaking.[110]

This leads to Wright's understanding that everything that is done *in the name of Jesus* and seeks to be part of 'building for the kingdom' is 'gospel work'. It solves instantly the conceptual problems that many have had with relating traditional 'evangelism' to the seeking of social justice and care for the environment and creation. None of these can be said to have priority because they all form part of the coming kingdom and God's renewal of creation. The commitment to promoting all of these aspects of the kingdom is therefore integral to being a 'gospel' Christian.[111]

Idolatry

Some scholars tend to emphasize Hellenism (Greek thought) as the major influence upon Paul. Against this, Wright argues that Paul possessed a thoroughly Jewish theology re-thought around his recognition of Jesus as the Messiah.[112] Standing firmly within this Jewish tradition, the major thrust of Paul's polemic was not against Judaism but the pagan world and its idolatry.[113] Central to Paul's missionary preaching was the calling to the Gentiles to exchange this idolatry, with its multiplicity of gods, divinization of created things and consequent path towards dehumanization and self-destruction, for worship of the one, living, creator God (see 1 Thessalonians 1.9–10).[114] Through the death and resurrection of the Jewish Messiah, Paul declared, this God had announced Jesus to be Lord of the world and the one to whom Gentiles were now summoned to the obedience of faith. This meant that the Gentiles could now receive God's Spirit, join God's single family and find their way, alongside Jews, to that fully human way of living of which paganism was just a parody.[115] The key term that Paul used to describe the process by which people became Christians was 'call', as they heard God's Word announcing the resurrection of Jesus and were moved by the Holy Spirit to believe this message and respond.[116] Paul's language of 'justification', Wright argues, possessed a closely related but rather different and more specific meaning.[117]

Victory

In explaining Paul's perspective on the death of Jesus and the atonement, Wright argues for the priority of 'the victory model', presenting Jesus' death as winning a mighty victory over the enemies of sin and evil.[118] Once again this is through a major emphasis upon the importance that Paul attached to the story of Israel, particularly the role of the law and Jesus' role as Israel's representative Messiah (against the commonly held view that the title 'Christ' had little or no messianic significance for Paul).[119] The law was a vital part of

God's covenant plan to work through Israel to redeem the world, and one of Paul's central insights, shown especially in Romans, was the strange 'negative but positive' role that it had in this process. Promising life, both through its commandments and by keeping Israel separate from the world, the law actually worked to 'increase the trespass' by somehow drawing the whole of the world's sin to its height in Israel (Romans 5.20; 7.7–25).[120] Once drawn onto Israel, however, this sin could be passed on to her representative king, Jesus the Messiah, whose death on the cross then enabled God to execute his judgement upon this sin and totally condemn it (Romans 8.3).[121] This evil was allowed to do its worst but through this very process the principalities and powers behind it were exhausted and disarmed; this brought about their full defeat and the rolling back of evil throughout the cosmos through the arrival of God's new age (Colossians 2.15).[122] The significance of this may go beyond God's forgiveness of personal sin but this is very much included within it. Jesus' status as the Messiah/ Christ means that all those Jews and Gentiles who belong to him, through the inclusive means of baptism and faith, are therefore 'in Christ' and joined to Jesus in his death and resurrection. Brought about by the Holy Spirit, this is the means by which their sins are forgiven and they are enabled to live a renewed life within a world being similarly remade.

This understanding of the atonement therefore integrates a model of personal forgiveness completely within a much broader under-standing of the death of Jesus as God's answer to the power of evil in its entirety.[123] Completely maintaining the reality of God's wrath and judgement, this understanding also removes any sense of God having an internal conflict of attitudes towards us, since the death of Jesus reveals that it is sin that God hates, while loving human beings without reservation. This leads to Wright's suggestion that saying that 'the *love* of God is satisfied' is more helpful in understanding the death of Jesus and the atonement than talking in a similar way about God's wrath.[124]

Righteousness

Wright's understanding of 'the righteousness of God' is key to his interpretation of Paul's theology. Rather than indicating an abstract quality of God, Wright sees this concept as a very specific reference to God's faithfulness to his covenant promises to work through Israel to address the problem of evil.[125] Unpacking the derivation of this metaphor from its law court setting, Wright argues for a clear distinction to be made between when 'righteousness' is used of God and when it is used of people. Used of God, it refers to the impartiality associated with the judge deciding a case, his being true to the law, his helping the poor and vulnerable and his dealing properly with evil. Used of people, it refers to their status (as guilty or not guilty) once God has delivered his verdict.[126] For biblically minded first-century Jews, all of this was seen in terms of God's covenant with Israel, with YHWH commonly expected to fulfil those aspects of his righteousness by rescuing and vindicating Israel and destroying the Gentiles. Such a covenantal reading thus formed a vital second layer of the law court reading of righteousness. Paul understood all these same aspects of God's righteousness to have been fulfilled in and through Jesus, though surprisingly and in a way that had not been expected.

According to Wright, Paul's letter to the Romans particularly centres on the problem of how God could fulfil his 'righteousness'/'covenant faithfulness', once Israel herself, as the supposed bearer of his solution to the plight of the world, had failed to live up to this calling. Rather than seek to be a blessing to the nations, Israel had instead sought to establish a 'righteousness' exclusive to Israel (the meaning of 'a righteousness of her own' in Romans 10.3). Caught up in sin, like the rest of the world, Israel's vocation had thus been rendered useless, appearing to place the whole of the covenant plan in jeopardy (Romans 1—3.20).[127] Now, however, Paul then goes on to declare, God had provided the solution, revealing his 'righteousness' through the faithfulness (to this covenant purpose) of Jesus as Israel's Messiah (Romans 3.21–22a). Wright describes the death of Jesus the Messiah as 'the climax of the covenant' since it both dealt with the problem of evil and demonstrated God's impartiality, by enabling Gentiles as well as Jews to enter the single people of God (Romans 3.22b–31).[128] In the rest of Romans, Paul unpacks how this outcome had always been part of God's covenant plan (Romans 4, 7, 9—11), the blessings now to be received in Jesus the Messiah (Romans 5, 8) and the implications of all this for how the one Church of Gentiles and Jews now needed to live in response to this (Romans 6, 12—16).[129]

Justification

As a consequence of all this, Wright has proposed a rather different understanding of 'justification by faith'. An important part of this is Wright's rejection (along with others from the so-called 'new perspective') of the view that Judaism was concerned with *earning* God's salvation through 'works of the law'. 'Works of the law' were instead understood as the God-given means for members of the covenant to demonstrate their loyalty to him and were therefore seen as the *present* marker of those people whom God would 'declare righteous/not guilty' (or 'justify') *on that future day* when he acted to restore his world.[130]

Paul's understanding of the significance of Jesus, however, and his altered perspective upon the role of the law within God's covenant plan, now changed all this. The sole markers in the present of those whom God would 'justify' in the future were faith in Jesus the Messiah and the 'new covenant' sign of baptism which incorporated believers into the Messiah's death and resurrection.[131] Fundamental to both faith and baptism was their thoroughly inclusive nature which demonstrated that belonging to the people of God had now become open to absolutely everyone (Galatians 3.26–29).[132]

This is what made Paul so opposed, particularly in Galatians, towards those within the church who insisted that Gentiles needed to be circumcised to enter the people of God. To Paul this was heresy because it denied the gospel truth that God had fulfilled his covenant purpose in Jesus by setting Israel free from the curse of the law and inviting everyone to become his one, undivided people.[133] All the parts of the Jewish law that had been designed to establish a barrier between Jews and Gentiles (such as circumcision and food laws) were now obsolete and any attempt to re-establish them as boundary markers was to re-enter the curse of the law and, ironically, adopt something similar to the tribal exclusivity and consequent idolatry associated with paganism (Galatians 4.8–10).[134]

Wright has therefore, highly controversially, redefined the doctrine of 'justification by faith' as being principally about ecclesiology (how we should recognize the Church) rather than soteriology (how we are saved).[135] He has also turned a doctrine more commonly applied than any other to exclude people from being 'proper Christians' into one that refuses to sanction the use of any boundary markers other than baptism and faith in Jesus the Messiah. Wright argues that he has rejected very little within the previous understanding of 'justification' and 'the gospel' – he just doesn't believe that the New Testament is speaking of these things when it uses these terms. It is far more specific with regard to the former and far broader in the meaning it attaches to the latter. One consequence of Wright's insistence on distinguishing God's 'righteousness' from ours is his rejection of 'imputed righteousness' (the idea that through the death of Jesus, God transfers *his* righteousness to us). This, Wright argues, is based upon a misreading of texts and key technical terms, which results in a confusion of categories. It is also unnecessary, given the Pauline emphasis upon everyone 'in the Messiah' being regarded by God as having died with him, been vindicated through his resurrection, and adopted as his children.[136]

Son of God

Wright's stress upon the story of Israel being critical to understanding Jesus leads to his insistence upon the proper process by which the title 'Son of God' should be understood. In the Old Testament 'Son of God' referred, in the first instance, to Israel herself (Exodus 4.22; Hosea 11.1), and then to her representative Messiah (2 Samuel 7.14; Psalms 2.7; 89.27). 'Son of God' as a title for Jesus, was one therefore that *initially* spoke of him having a crucial role in God's purposes rather than indicating a divine being.[137] It also contained an important element of polemic against a pagan culture in which the phrase 'Son of God' was commonly used to refer to the Roman Emperor.

From this basis, however, Wright goes on to emphasize that the very high Christology that people have usually associated with the phrase 'Son of God' is strongly present in Paul, without losing the 'Israel' and 'Messiah' meanings. Like the writers of the Gospels, Paul understood Jesus, as Israel's Messiah, to have brought in his own person the fulfilment of God's promises, leading him to declare that 'God was in the Messiah reconciling the world to himself'.[138] This was followed by a further recognition that the risen Jesus had been exalted to share the glory of the one God because he had done what only God could do (Philippians 2.5–11).

From this context, Paul completely rethought his understanding of God. Remaining fiercely monotheistic, he redefined this monotheism by taking some of the most emphatic statements of God's oneness from the Old Testament (particularly 'the Shema' in Deuteronomy 6.4–5) and incorporating Jesus within them (see 1 Corinthians 8.4–6).[139] Without losing any of its original messianic and representative sense, 'Son of God' therefore took on a much deeper layer of meaning for Paul, signifying Jesus' status as God's 'second self' and ultimate self-expression as a human being.

The Spirit

The Holy Spirit also played a crucial role within Paul's presentation of the fresh understanding of God. The Spirit was incorporated, alongside the Messiah, into monotheistic statements from the Old Testament and Paul used 'the Spirit' and 'the Messiah' interchangeably in describing the saving actions of the one God (see Romans 8.9–11, for example).[140] Rather than this being in tension with the belief in the oneness of God, the creational and covenantal nature of Jewish monotheism facilitated this move towards a Trinitarian understanding through the ease with which it already spoke of the one God being present through his wisdom, glory or law.[141]

Wright argues that this rethinking of the nature of God was something that Paul did completely consciously. Just as Israel's God had been revealed in a new way as YHWH through the exodus from Egypt (Exodus 3), so Paul understood this same God to have now been revealed in a full and final way through the greater exodus achieved through the death and resurrection of his Son and the work of his Spirit.[142] Paul was therefore fully conscious that the unity in diversity that he called the one Church to express was a direct reflection of the unity in diversity revealed within the one God (1 Corinthians 12.4–6).[143]

Lord

Wright affirms that Paul's use of the title 'Lord' for Jesus was a deliberate aspect of this rethinking of God, given that 'Lord' in the Septuagint (the Greek translation of the Old Testament) was used to translate YHWH. Developing the thought of other recent writers, Wright has gone on to emphasize how politically subversive it was for Christians to proclaim that 'Jesus is Lord'.[144] Once again this exegesis is set firmly within both the story of the Old Testament, with its constant critique of oppressive pagan power, and first-century historical context, when worship of the Roman Emperor was the fastest-growing religion.[145] Against this background Wright has pointed to the very direct challenge that 'Jesus is Lord' made to Rome and its imperial ideology, summing this up with the phrase that 'if Jesus Christ is Lord then Caesar isn't!'

This, in turn, has produced a far more political reading of Paul's letters. Wright emphasizes how much, especially within Philippians and Romans, should be read as encoded but clear messages to the Christians in those places to locate their security and identity in Jesus the Messiah rather than in Caesar.[146] In both letters Paul very deliberately takes titles and slogans used to bolster Caesar's power and gives these to Jesus instead. Romans 13.1–7 is then read very differently with its statements about obedience to rulers understood within the context of the description as God's servants established by (and therefore accountable to) him.[147] Wright has also highlighted the deeply political nature of the Gospels, with Luke 2 demonstrating a similar transfer of 'Caesar titles' to Jesus and the subversive nature of Jesus' kingship being drawn out more strongly than has often been recognized.[148]

Wright does much the same in relation to the Acts of the Apostles. The strongly political implications of the Ascension of Jesus are shown by its imperial parallels based upon the common recognition that 'the one who reigns in heaven, rules on earth.'[149] This theme continues through Acts, the climax of its first half being the downfall of the Jewish King Herod Agrippa after he persecutes the Church and then claims an authority that belongs only to God (Acts 12).[150] The second half of Acts, with its account of the spread of the Gentile mission, goes on to climax in a startling parallel. Seeking to take the gospel to Rome, Paul is furiously resisted by almost every force of evil but is eventually successful, proclaiming, 'right under the Emperor's nose', the kingdom of God and the Lord Jesus Christ 'boldly and unhindered' (Acts 27—28).[151]

All this radically challenges any understanding that Christians should be politically quietist. To proclaim the good news that 'Jesus is Lord', Wright argues, always includes a very direct challenge to the power of evil, including its modern-day 'imperial' forms, because it proclaims to these powers that with the arrival of God's kingdom their 'time is up'.[152] A properly Christian eschatology, therefore, will always be political while also being radically distinct in its refusal to use evil's weapons and its rejection of disorder, which simply replaces one form of oppression with another.[153] To deny such a political agenda, Wright argues, is to follow the second-century Gnostics rather than authentic Christianity. It was Christians reading those books that now form the New Testament who were being persecuted and put to death by the Romans in the early years of Christianity because their message was rightly seen as deeply subversive. The last thing any tyrant or emperor would feel threatened by were Gnostic 'Christians' reading the 'Gospel of Thomas' or 'Gospel of Judas', whose 'hope' had become that of a disembodied escape from the world rather than being part of the kingdom coming 'on earth as it is in heaven'.[154]

Wright's challenge here is as much to those who have insisted on a low Christology alongside 'political readings' of the New Testament as to those who have maintained a high Christology alongside non-political readings. To proclaim that 'Jesus is Lord', with the full rethinking of God that this phrase implies, provides more political challenge to the present structures of power within this world than anything else.[155]

Parousia/appearing

This counter-imperial emphasis also forms an important element within Paul's references to the Messiah's future 'parousia' or 'presence'. Once again such language was in regular contemporary use, describing visits to territories by their kings and emperors.[156] Combining this language with eschatological imagery from the Old Testament, Paul presented the future presence of the Messiah as bringing to fulfilment the Day of YHWH and the completion of his project to restore creation. Wright particularly emphasizes the New Testament's use of the term 'appearing' (used in this context in Colossians 3.4 and 1 John 3.2) in order to draw attention to its integrated cosmology of heaven and earth and the sense of drawing back a previously unnoticed curtain to see the Messiah 'face to face'.[157] At this point the whole of creation will be renewed as it is flooded with God's presence. The resurrection of those who have died 'in the Messiah' will occur, along with the transformation of those Christians still living, and both will be given new bodies so that they can fulfil God's commission to rule his earth and enjoy it for ever.[158]

Wright emphatically opposes, therefore, any idea that believers will then be taken off to 'heaven', and the common description of 'heaven' as 'our real home'.[159] New Testament passages that speak of a salvation 'kept in heaven for you' (1 Peter 1.4) and 'storing up riches in heaven' (Matthew 6.19–21) are, by contrast, referring to a reality presently hidden that will later be revealed and enjoyed here, as the joining of heaven and earth becomes full and final.[160] Paul's statement in Philippians 3.20 about Christians having their 'citizenship in heaven' is understood in a similar manner through its parallel to Roman citizens within Philippi who were looking for the Emperor's future presence within their colony rather than expecting one day to go and live with him in Rome.[161] Passages such as John 14.1–6 and Luke 23.43 are then explicable as descriptions of the temporary or interim state in paradise that Jesus' followers will possess ahead of his 'appearing', their future resurrection and the joining of the 'new heavens' and 'new earth'.[162]

Judgement

Wright emphasizes that belief in a future judgement is indispensable to any understanding of God's goodness and justice.[163] He is also clear that this judgement by the Messiah will be in accordance with the entirety of the life that has been led (see Romans 14.9–10; 2 Corinthians 5.10).[164] Despite the clarity of these and other passages, this idea has been controversial; some have suggested that 'judgement according to deeds' is a denial of grace and 'justification by faith'.[165] In response, Wright argues that justification by faith is the Spirit's bringing forward of that eschatological verdict into the present, based upon the first fruit of that expected change which is people possessing the faith to proclaim that 'Jesus is Lord'.[166] Wright also draws attention to the judgement of the deeds of Christians on 'the Day of the Lord', with work that is built upon the foundation of Jesus the Messiah lasting into the new creation while work that is not is burnt up (1 Corinthians 3.10–17).[167] In addressing the fate of those people who are not found 'in the Messiah', Wright rejects both the idea of a hell of endless torment and the concept of annihilation. Instead he suggests that the fate of the lost is to continue existing but with the loss of any remaining image of God within them. Those who have rejected Jesus will eventually, therefore, have this choice confirmed as they cease to be fully and genuinely human.[168] Once this process of judgement has been completed, the Messiah will hand over this kingdom to the Father, who will then be 'all in all' as God's creation reaches that point at which it is completely restored.

The Church

Wright understands the calling of the people of God as being to live in the light of Easter by seeking to anticipate in the present as much as possible of this future resurrection life.[169] Living on earth as 'citizens of heaven', the Church's role is to proclaim that Jesus is Lord. It does this through its words and deeds imagining and embodying the reality of the 'new creation' that Jesus Christ has come to bring. It is clarity over its final destination, therefore, that is vital to the Church thinking clearly about the nature of its worship and mission.

The Holy Spirit is the one who makes all this happen. Wright describes the Spirit's role in eschatological terms bringing not only God's presence but also the reality of his future age into the present world order (the 'advance payment').[170] This enables the Church to implement the achievement of Jesus and be the channel of his salvation coming further into the world.[171] It is the Spirit, therefore, who works through Christian 'heralds' to call people through the proclamation of the gospel and to make them respond with faith. As they do so, the Spirit then brings these people, through baptism, into the Body of the Messiah, thus incorporating them within that part of God's new creation that has already been established (2 Corinthians 5.17).[172] From this point, the Spirit is the one who inspires the Church and individual Christians to produce further signs of God's new world within the present one, anticipating their future reign over the earth as its 'priests and rulers' (Romans 5.17; Revelation 22).[173] Wright describes this dual role as 'priests and rulers' as being to sum up the praise of creation to God and reflect God's rule to the world. One particular implication of this is the Church being able to exercise within itself that judgement that it will one day have over the new creation (1 Corinthians 6.1–8).[174] Another advance sign of the new creation that the Church is called to display is the unity of its people across the normal divisions within the world of class, race and gender. This, more than anything else, strikes terror into divisive powers of evil through its declaration that 'their time is up' (Ephesians 3.10).[175]

Wright therefore sees a very rich ecclesiology (doctrine of the church) contained within the New Testament and argues that allegiance to the visible, historical Church is part of allegiance to the gospel itself.[176] Paying attention to both the story of Israel and God's purpose for the world are the vital steps to appreciating this. Wright also suggests that the reluctance on the part of liberal Protestantism to engage with such ecclesiology has been the major factor influencing its denial of the Pauline authorship of Ephesians and Colossians.[177] He adds that evangelicalism has often, in practice, been seeking to do something very similar through its insistence on making Romans and Galatians primary for reconstructing Pauline theology. As a corrective to this, Wright proposes that the best overall grasp of Pauline theology is probably gained by seeking to locate its various elements within the broad picture of the scope of salvation provided by Ephesians, the authenticity of which there is no good reason to doubt.[178]

Virtue

Central to the way in which the Holy Spirit prepares and equips believers for the new creation and their role as its priests and rulers (including their current worship and mission) is through their development of Christian 'character' or 'virtue'. The whole basis of Christian ethics is, therefore, eschatological and vocational, with eternal life being not an arbitrary 'reward' but the outcome of believers learning to live within the new world they will one day inherit.[179] Fundamental to this is the recognition that because Christians are already joined by the Spirit to the Messiah's resurrection body and because their own bodies will one day be raised, what they do with these bodies in the present really matters (1 Corinthians 6.12–20).[180]

In his explanation of the New Testament perspective on ethics, Wright draws some parallels to the way in which Aristotle charted the path towards his understanding of the goal of human living ('flourishing'). For Aristotle this goal could be reached by the cultivation of certain strengths so that these virtues eventually became habitual.[181]

Transcending this with its goal of a redeemed humanity living within a new creation, together with a number of 'strengths' that Aristotle undervalued (such as love, meekness and humility), Wright insists that the New Testament contains a very similar emphasis on the need for sustained discipline and effort to develop these virtues. All brought about by God's grace and the action of the Spirit, the supreme Christian virtues are faith, hope and especially love, because these are the things that will last into the new creation and therefore form 'bridges' into it from the present world order (1 Corinthians 13).[182] This gives further explanation to the nature of the Sermon on the Mount, understanding Jesus' command to 'be perfect/complete' (Matthew 5.48) as the exhortation to start living more like the people that we will one day be remade into by God.[183] The command for Christians to forgive also anticipates our future liberation from the effect of evil committed against us.[184]

Christian living is not, therefore, about obeying rules. Rules might point to good ways of living but they lack both the power to bring about such good living and also much in the way of a truly positive vision. Rules also tend not to possess the flexibility to be really specific to the situations we face.[185] Neither, at the opposite extreme, is Christian living about being released to do 'what comes naturally'.[186] Instead, Wright argues that Christian living is about the sustained effort (coming very unnaturally at first) to live within the new creation that the Spirit has brought. This involves constantly taking decisions that eventually become habitual and steadily lead to the Spirit's renewal of our minds so that our lives are gradually more conformed to God's will. Rather than this hard work being a sign of hypocrisy or 'lack of authenticity', it is the means of allowing the Spirit to draw more of God's future into the present reality of our lives.[187]

Wright makes a close link between the development of such virtue and the role of God's people in becoming a royal priesthood, exercising God's rule over the world. Responsibility for a redeemed creation in the future means that such redemption must be steadily more present within our own bodies.[188] Included within this is the call to undergo suffering. As the Spirit enables Christians to embody in their suffering the dying and rising of the Messiah, they then become part of the victory that Jesus achieved on the cross. Not only, says Wright, will Christian living always involve a struggle, it will often involve an apparent defeat but with the promise that 'if we endure we will reign with him' (2 Timothy 2.12).[189]

The sacraments

'Worship' is therefore about the Church being led by the Spirit to live in ways that anticipate the reality of God's future age. Within this context, Wright argues that the sacraments are to be understood as special points, established by Jesus and used by the Holy Spirit to bring God's presence and new creation into the world.[190]

Such a sacramental theology is based on the biblical world-view of heaven and earth being understood as interlocking dimensions of the created order rather than distant from one another. It also rests upon continuity with the presentation of salvation in the Old Testament and the process towards God's ultimate intention to fill the whole of the world with his presence (Isaiah 11.9). This was anticipated by the establishment of the Temple as the place where heaven and earth were joined and YHWH could be met (1 Kings 8) and the connection made, particularly in Isaiah, between the future renewal of the covenant and the renewal of creation (Isaiah 54—55). Framed between his baptism and the Last Supper, Jesus' ministry, particularly the words and actions that showed that he regarded the Temple as being replaced by his own person (see Matthew 12.6), indicated this coming of YHWH's presence. This presence was more fully established by Jesus' resurrection, his Ascension and the sending of the Spirit.[191] Rather than the sacraments being 'bare signs' of salvation, Wright argues that the Spirit instead enables them to be 'effective signs' of this salvation, given to bring the Messiah's risen body, as that part of God's creation that has already been renewed, into the world.[192]

Another important aspect of the sacraments, according to Wright, is the way God can use time, being able to collapse past, present and future into single moments.[193] The Passover meal looked back to Israel's rescue from Egypt, and on to her ultimate liberation; so the Eucharist brings both the significance of Jesus' past death and something of God's future renewal of the cosmos into the present to nourish and equip the Church. Like the fruit brought back from the promised land by the Israelite spies, Holy Communion is thus given to sustain the Church as it travels towards God's promised future.

Baptism similarly brings God's past creation, his saving actions and his future new creation into the present by joining us to the risen Jesus and enfolding our story within that of God's salvation of the world.[194]

The ordinary and earthly nature of the sacraments is an indispensable sign of the goal of Christian salvation being a renewed and transformed earth, rather than escape from it. This understanding of baptism and the Eucharist in turn points to a world full of sacramental possibilities, as every good thing that God has created can potentially anticipate the new creation and become a channel of the presence of the risen Jesus.[195] Within this context Wright also affirms the sacramental nature of marriage through its reflection of the coming together of heaven and earth in the new creation, and many of the Church's traditional liturgical actions as a further drawing out of what happens in baptism.[196]

In addition, Wright pays particular attention to the way in which the Eucharist equips the Church for holistic mission in the world. Precisely because this mission is battling 'principalities and powers' rather than 'flesh and blood', nourishment by the fruit of the new creation is vital for a Church that seeks to be an agent of this new creation.[197] Such a connection encourages those who recognize Jesus in the breaking of bread also to recognize him sacramentally in the suffering and poor people that they help and care for (Matthew 25.31–46).

Prayer

Similarly, Wright explains the significance of prayer in terms of the overlap of earth and heaven, and God's new creation being able to enter into the old. Caught in this overlap of ages, followers of Jesus in the present can see this future age only 'through a glass darkly', as both we and creation itself groan for rebirth. The Spirit therefore has a crucial role in praying for and through Christians, particularly from those places where the world is most in pain, so that more of God's future can come forward into the present to meet us (Romans 8.26–27).[198] Wright particularly emphasizes the role of the Church to 'groan with prayer' from the midst of a hurting world rather than 'be smug on the sidelines', speaking of the Church having the priestly vocation of standing before God with creation on its heart.[199]

Understanding the Lord's Prayer as a reflection of what Jesus was doing within his ministry, Wright sees it as a prayer for followers of Jesus to be joined to him in this kingdom movement.[200] Christian prayer, rather than enabling people to be heard by a distant deity, forms the vital means of the inner life of God, which we will share in the future, being able to enter into the present lives of Christian believers.

The authority of God exercised through Scripture

With regard to the Bible's authority, Wright suggests that this term should be understood as shorthand for 'the authority of God exercised through Scripture'.[201] Rejecting alternative models of scriptural authority that in reality place the locus of that authority elsewhere (including evangelical tradition), Wright argues that the nature of Scripture should be allowed to guide the understanding of its authority and how this operates. Scripture is the story of the sovereign exercise of God's authority over his creation, usually through people delegated to act, speak or write proclaiming this authority.[202] Resisting any sense that its writers 'didn't know they were writing Scripture', Wright asserts that the writings found in the Bible were very consciously written to effect God's authority, which is exercised today through the retelling of Scripture's story, including the summons to live within its narrative. The Bible, rather than being an inspired commentary on the way in which salvation works, is therefore an integral part of God's plan for actually bringing in the new creation. Through the power of its retelling of the mighty acts of God, from creation to new creation, the Bible is able to confront, undermine and replace alternative world-views with their rival narratives and authority claims.[203]

The fifth act

The Church's task is to continue retelling Scripture's story and by so doing to live within this story and issue God's summons to the world to live within it as well. Critical to this is the recognition of the different stages of the Bible's story, which Wright likens to the different acts of a five-act play. The first four acts are 'Creation', 'Fall', 'Israel' and 'Jesus'; the fifth act is 'The Church'. Just the first scene of this 'fifth act' is contained in the Bible, together with an indication of how the whole story will finish (in Romans 8, 1 Corinthians 15 and parts of Revelation).[204] Rather than being encouraged to repeat earlier parts of the story, the Church is called to soak itself within the whole of the Bible's story so that, led by the Holy Spirit, it can 'faithfully improvise its performance' within the fifth act in the light of where the overall story has come from and where it is heading. The Bible, in announcing God's authority, therefore has the crucial role in leading the Church to proclaim this authority through the lordship of Jesus; by so doing it plays its role in the further coming of God's kingdom, 'on earth as it is in heaven'.[205]

A summary of the overall paradigm shift that Wright is proposing

This last point is probably the best path into attempting to sum up in a few sentences the overall paradigm shift that Wright is proposing in how to understand Jesus and the New Testament. In its reading of the New Testament, the Christian Church needs to shed the dualist lens introduced by the Gnostics (and reinforced by the Enlightenment) that seeks to detach matters of faith and 'spirituality' from the physical world in which we live. This will involve the recovery of a properly Jewish theology of creation that will enable us to understand Jesus as coming to inaugurate that new creation and renew the world rather than destroy it. Rather than restricting the gospel to being about individuals 'going to heaven when you die', the Church's role is to live within the story of Scripture, demonstrating, by word and deed, radical and Spirit-filled signs of the resurrection life that Jesus Christ has come to bring. This will make it clear that the summons to belong to Jesus, live under his lordship and become part of this life is for everything and everyone.

4

Tom Wright's theology in a pastoral context

————•─•─•────

The previous chapter has gone some distance to showing how the scholarship of Tom Wright has provided convincing responses to many of the issues raised in the second chapter of this book. It has not been intended to suggest that these are the only important theological issues or that they indeed have been entirely resolved. My hope, nonetheless, is that its contents will encourage readers to approach Wright's work with a greater degree of confidence as they seek answers to the specific questions and issues with which they themselves are grappling.

The purpose of the rest of this book is to give further encouragement to this process by outlining some of the ways in which the theology of Tom Wright has made a difference to the life and ministry of the church of which I am vicar. Built in 1866, Christ Church, New Malden has always stood firmly within the evangelical tradition of the Church of England with a particularly strong commitment to biblical preaching and mission. In recent years Christ Church has been dramatically reshaped to respond to its twenty-first-century context, and much of this change has been strongly influenced by the theology of Tom Wright. Incomplete and still very much 'work in progress', my hope is that this ongoing story will illustrate the clarity and confidence that can be gained in church life once leaders and congregations start engaging with Wright's theology and exploring its practical implications. Subsequent chapters look at 'mission' and 'church life' more generally; this chapter focuses on what happens if a 'new heavens, new earth' eschatology makes its way into the pastoral theology and practice of the local church.

Ministry around the time of death and bereavement

As for many clergy, responding to death and bereavement and the surrounding issues is an important part of my job. The most obvious manifestation of this, typical for a Church of England vicar, is the regular number of funeral services that my colleagues and I are called upon to take. The majority of these funerals are of members of the parish (the geographical area assigned to our church) who are not churchgoers, but their next of kin have nevertheless asked for a Church of England service. In most cases the deceased is someone I have never met. Alongside the funerals for church members, these services sometimes take place at church but more often at one of the local cemeteries or crematoriums. Sometimes these services involve a burial but, as throughout much of the UK, it is far more common for the body to be cremated.

My usual practice and that of my team is to visit the family of the deceased before the service, usually at their home, offering pastoral care as well as in order to gather information about the life of the deceased and plan the service. Together with the service itself and the 'after-care' following the funeral, this area of ministry has proved to be one of the most deeply rewarding that I have undertaken. The opportunity and indeed privilege to minister to people at a time of such obvious need forms one of many reasons why I am delighted to be part of the Church of England.

Needless to say, handling death and bereavement on such a regular basis throws up a number of really important issues, one of the most sensitive of these being the future hope. Tom Wright has commented on the strength of response that writing on this subject can provoke.[1] Wright was probably thinking most obviously when he wrote this of the reaction from right-wing evangelicals in the USA with their 'dispensational premillennialism'. This term describes the belief of those who, on the basis of their reading of 1 Thessalonians 4, Revelation 20 and Matthew 24 (and its parallels in Mark and Luke), believe in a very literal understanding of a 'rapture', 'tribulation' and the 'thousand-year reign of Christ'. To many such Christians, any questioning of this understanding of 'the Christian hope', together with its frequently associated Zionism (belief in the literal fulfilment of God's Old Testament promises for the modern state of Israel), can indeed provoke the strongest of responses. Though rarer in the UK, these beliefs can be found in some evangelical churches, requiring a careful response to their specific issues. The sensitive nature of the question of 'the Christian future hope' for everyone, however, especially around the time of death and bereavement, means that the relevance of Wright's comment goes well beyond this particular grouping.

In particular, I have found within my very English and 'suburban' setting that both Christians and non-Christians do expect the message of hope that I present to be about 'going to heaven when you die'. Understandably concerned about the destination of their loved one, this often results in the desire for a message that combines a virtual universalism (the belief that everyone will be 'saved', unless they have been particularly bad) with the reassurance that the deceased has gone to 'a better place' and is now out of suffering and pain. The other seemingly distinct feature is that many bereaved families wish a very full tribute to the deceased, marking those aspects of their life which they particularly valued, to form a major part of the funeral. The 'tribute address' given by Earl Spencer at the funeral of Diana, Princess of Wales in 1997 played a significant role in accelerating this expectation, with most families now wanting either to make similar 'tributes' themselves, or that these sentiments form the main substance of the address that is given.[2]

Engagement with this latter area of need has facilitated my presentation at funerals of the hope of resurrection and 'new heavens, new earth'. Including (and indeed usually delivering) a warm and generous tribute towards 'all that was good' in the deceased's life has enabled this to be placed within the context of a very strong and positive theology of creation that affirms with thanksgiving all the good things God has given us. Rather than just focusing upon good memories, such a tribute can also acknowledge the more difficult aspects of the deceased's life, and this can sometimes form an important part of responding to the pastoral needs of those grieving. If carefully done, it can be possible to include some acknowledgement (sometimes 'encoded') of the deceased's faults and weaknesses. All this then prepares the way extremely well for a presentation of the Christian hope that uses the resurrection of Jesus to declare the certainty of God's promise to one day completely restore a 'new creation' in which such difficulty, pain and sin will have no part. During this part of the address I deliberately build into this picture of 'new heavens, new earth' the presence and indeed enhancement of all the aspects of the goodness of creation that have been evident in the life of the deceased.

Two important notes are needed at this point. The first is that unless the person who has died made a profession of Christian faith, I make sure that this presentation of the Christian hope is general, rather than specific to the deceased and for those 'who place their faith in Jesus Christ'. If pressed by the family for an answer on their loved one's destination (which is rare) I always answer, with complete honesty, that I don't know. My regular experience, however, is that the warmth created by the positive engagement with the life of the deceased, the acknowledgement of their hardships and the clear integration of both within the message of hope presented, results in this question not being one they are determined to press. Surprisingly, perhaps, the grieving relatives usually appear prepared to leave this question of the destination of the deceased in God's hands and accept my emphasis upon the challenge to them of responding to the rich vision of Christian hope they have heard outlined.

The other point concerns the amount of continuity between our present and future lives that is envisaged within such a vision of the Christian hope. On a few occasions I have heard Tom Wright criticized for laying too great a stress on the continuity of this future to the present, given the emphasis within the New Testament upon a *new* heaven and *new* earth. This sentiment was expressed to me on one occasion by a member of my congregation who on hearing my explanation of our future hope declared with some disappointment, 'So are you saying this is all there is?' My response to such questions is to assert the utter goodness of the created order witnessed to by Genesis 1 and the best of our human experience, as the basis for a proper emphasis upon continuity within the new creation. I then add, however, that this emphasis upon continuity needs to be balanced with the discontinuity of a fallen earth that is set to be wonderfully transformed through being joined to a renewed heaven and completely purged of sin, death and suffering.

Responding to 'the hope of heaven'

All this, of course, means that a response is needed to those vast numbers of Christians previously receiving immense comfort from the belief that their loved ones who have died as Christian believers have now 'made it' by getting to heaven. This obviously requires sensitive handling. One means I have found helpful in doing this is by using the phrase, coined by Tom Wright himself, to describe the major focus of the New Testament hope being on 'life *after* life after death'.[3] This enables the major emphasis on 'new heavens, new earth' eschatology to be combined with the less central but nonetheless important biblical affirmation that those who have died as followers of Jesus have gone 'to be with the Lord'. Since Jesus is in heaven, affirming that 'the Christian departed' have 'gone to heaven' can perhaps be justified. But the fact that the Bible avoids this language, and the danger of reinforcing this as *the* Christian hope, has led me to prefer to use the language of believers 'going to be with Jesus' ahead of their future resurrection. I suggest that Philippians 1 and Luke 23.43 both imply that this existence 'with Jesus' is something fully conscious. I am also happy to affirm, with Wisdom 3.1–4, that 'the souls of the righteous are in God's hand', provided that 'soul' is understood to be referring to 'that about us which continues in God's care and presence' rather than the Platonic idea of the disembodied soul as the essential and therefore only permanent part of someone's being.[4]

While this still begs a number of questions that the New Testament doesn't answer, I have found that this understanding of the future hope does work to resolve a number of greater problems that Christians have with the traditional understanding of 'heaven' as their final destination. One aspect of this, occasionally expressed by those braver than most, is that the whole idea of 'heaven' as a permanent dwelling place can sound rather boring. The final line of 'Once in royal David's city' ('all in white shall wait around') shows that not all the blame for this can be placed on ancient paintings of angels sitting on clouds playing harps! Partly in response to this, a more recent tendency among younger evangelicals has been to present 'heaven' as a party, based upon those passages speaking of a future messianic banquet (Isaiah 25.6; Matthew 8.11; Luke 14.15). The weakness of this, however, was brought home to me some time ago through a comment from a young woman whose Christian father had died some years before. 'I know I'm meant to see heaven as an endless party,' she said, 'but the problem is that I can't imagine my dad enjoying that!' Her remark was symptomatic of a struggle to see proper fullness and reality in the picture of the Christian hope that her evangelical tradition had given her.

Just as problematic is the implication that because heaven is 'our real home', Christians should not be too attached to life here on earth. I remember my own grandmother saying as she was dying that she knew that she shouldn't want to stay on earth, but that was how she felt. While her ambivalence could perhaps be seen to be supported by Paul's comments in Philippians 1.21–24, her comment did cause me to reflect in later years upon a theology that had led her to feel guilty at wanting to continue living for God on earth and enjoying his good creation.

All these problems can be avoided through emphasizing that when Christians die they leave their pain and difficulty and 'go to be with Jesus', before that *future* day of resurrection when Jesus will return and they receive God's wonderfully restored creation to enjoy and take responsibility for. Following Wright's lead, I make it clear that rather than being passive, our role as 'rulers and priests' in the new creation will involve the richness of new tasks and opportunities.[5] The skills and talents we have been given and which we have put to God's service in this present life will be enhanced and given back so we can use them further to his glory. This produces a picture of the Christian hope that everyone can relate to, get excited about and then start working towards in our Christian discipleship now.

'New heavens, new earth' and children

Like many churches, Christ Church, New Malden places a major priority on ministry to children and young people. Particularly around the age of six or seven, the issue of 'what happens after death' becomes very real to children, raising a number of questions that their parents often struggle to answer. On a number of occasions I have been asked to make visits to chat to a younger child about these issues, usually with a parent intently noting my responses! What I seek to do in these situations is combine a message declaring that we can trust God's love and fairness about what happens after death with a vision of his 'big plan' to one day recreate the world into a place where everything bad has been swept away and we can be part of helping him for ever.

I commonly find that such a vision of 'new heavens, new earth' makes a very strong connection with children's grasp of the goodness of creation and intuitive sense of 'what the world should be like'. I then seek to build on this in school assemblies and 'all-age' talks at church. On one occasion I used the illustration of a vast and impressive Lego castle that one of our young boys had taken ages to make. 'Did anything go wrong when you were making this?' I asked him. 'Yes, quite a few times,' he replied. 'Then why didn't you throw the whole thing away?' I asked, to which the boy responded by speaking with some indignation about how valuable and important his castle was. 'And so it is with God and this world,' I went on, explaining that the world is so precious to God that rather than 'chucking it away' when it went wrong, he was committed instead to completely restoring and renewing it. Such a message works equally well with adults and can be combined with an affirmation of the present world, more associated with 'liberalism', with no lessening at all of the more 'evangelical' emphasis on sin, its consequences, and the need for redemption. This can then serve as a very effective springboard for expounding some of the implications of 'new heavens, new earth' covered in the following chapters.

'New heavens, new earth' and ministry to those going through particular hardship

This eschatology has made significant impact in a pastoral context in its emphasis upon all the evil and injustice within this world being put right when Jesus returns. Reducing the Christian hope to 'going to heaven when you die' can very easily lend itself to the rather trite version of 'grin and bear it' that Karl Marx rightly reacted to. Speaking instead of the subversive nature of resurrection, and of Jesus reversing all the injustice and oppression within the world when he appears, puts a very different perspective on this. This, as we shall see in the following chapter, has major implications for Christian mission. But in a pastoral context I have found that it can carry tremendous significance in assuring those who have suffered unfairly (perhaps in the workplace or through other forms of structural unfairness and prejudice) that this injustice won't be either bypassed or forgotten when Jesus returns. Using the symbol of the millennium in Revelation 20, I have spoken of the way in which all injustice will be very deliberately put right during the reign of Jesus, as a crucial part of the process towards that complete renewal of his creation that God has promised to bring.[6] I have frequently found that this declaration of the certainty of God's future judgement upon such oppression makes a significant difference to people's ability to endure such evil and resist the temptation to return it.

Coming from a fairly conservative tradition of evangelicalism, a more 'charismatic' approach to healing and 'prayer ministry' is a relatively recent development at Christ Church. Like many evangelical churches, the arrival of such ministry has brought something of a tension between those enthusiastic for seeing 'signs and wonders' and others who are rather fearful of this. A factor that has helped here is Wright's emphasis upon heaven and earth as interlocking spheres of God's creation, with heaven understood as the 'control centre' for earth.[7] This has led to a rejection of the notion of 'miracles' where this term is understood to signify the intervention of a normally absent God.[8] The promotion of a more integrated cosmology has allowed such 'prayer ministry' to combine a strong expectation of God's action with a greater acceptance of the many different forms through which he might choose to do this. Prayer for God to act through things such as medical care and the help of others has thus been able to take its place alongside openness to the less explicable forms of healing that God also brings.

The place of redemptive suffering has been affirmed through this emphasis upon the continuous (if unseen) presence of God; this is much more difficult to achieve if God's 'intervention' is being constantly sought. With the affirmation that 'prayer always changes something', the vision of God's 'new creation' often breaking into this world *through* suffering has enabled a greater openness to the host of ways, alongside physical healing, that 'resurrection life' can become apparent. This has particularly included increased evidence of the fruit of the Spirit as people have sought to stay faithful to God through the hardships they have faced. This has then led to a deeper acceptance that some forms of healing will take place only when the 'new creation' is brought to completion.

An important pastoral question that this has raised is the extent to which physical and mental disability will be reversed in the new creation. The perspective that tended to regard all such disabilities as being one day 'healed' is now increasingly giving way to the assertion that this aspect of people's identity needs to be affirmed rather than seen as a problem to be resolved. Conscious of the dangers here, I seek to avoid dogmatism either way, laying a common emphasis upon the end of frustration, difficulty and prejudice in the new creation and the opportunity, for all of us, to thrive in the way God intended when he created us. This vision then provides a basis for us seeking to pray more of that future into the present as well.

Remaining problems . . .

As already mentioned, Tom Wright himself has said that 'going to heaven when you die' is so deeply entrenched as the Christian understanding of our future hope that he sometimes despairs of ever being able to change this.[9] Having myself preached 'new heavens, new earth' and endeavoured to show its practical implications throughout the seven years of my ordained ministry, I already know how he feels! A major problem is that whatever progress one makes in this is frequently undermined by the numerous hymns, worship songs and even jokes told in church life ('You'll never get to heaven if you carry on like that') that constantly reinforce the traditional perspective.[10] New hymns and songs undoubtedly need to be written to reinforce a more biblical eschatology (and take their place alongside hymns that already do this, such as 'For all the saints'). But in my experience, what most reinforces people's grasp of 'new heavens, new earth' is when the preaching of it runs alongside the exploration and demonstration of its practical implications for mission. To these we now turn.

5

Tom Wright's theology in a mission context

———◆◆◆———

Like many evangelical churches, Christ Church, New Malden has always possessed a strong emphasis upon the importance of what might be described as classical evangelism: preaching that is aimed at encouraging awareness of sin, repentance and a personal decision to turn to Christ as saviour. Throughout its history a clear understanding of the status of this as 'gospel ministry' has been a key factor motivating the energy and commitment that has sustained this work. This has resulted in a number of parish missions and the planting of two mission halls, which later became churches. In more recent times this has led to the adoption of the Alpha course and the development of a whole new Sunday service at 9.30 a.m. aimed at bringing newcomers into a relationship with Jesus Christ.[1] Beyond the parish, these same factors have resulted in an equally strong tradition of sending out mission partners to make Jesus known in other parts of the country and overseas.

Less theological confidence has existed, however, in relation to those aspects of the mission of Christ Church that could be described as 'social outreach'. A good amount of such work has been strongly encouraged by Christ Church over many years, through people such as missionary nurses abroad and various projects within the church and its surrounding area. However, this energy and commitment has not generally resulted in any clarity over the theological status of such work. Two statements made during my time at the church have particularly summed this up. One came from a returning missionary who, in the course of explaining her work, said to the congregation, 'I just don't feel that I can share the gospel with people unless I love them first.' The other was when one of our most energetic members involved in social outreach was heard to say, 'Maybe I'm a heretic but I believe that God mainly wants us to love people.' Both comments summed up the way in which those involved in such ministry combined an instinctive sense of God's calling them to a crucial work with uncertainty over its status in regard to 'the gospel'. Few people, after all, were being directly 'saved for heaven' through this work and so a sense remained that it was, at best, 'pre-gospel' ministry. Attempts to challenge this understanding tended to create a measure of discomfort, usually accompanied by warnings against the dangers of losing the necessary and primary emphasis upon personal conversion and drifting towards a liberal 'social gospel'.

'New heavens, new earth' and holistic mission

It is here that the effects of engaging with Tom Wright's theology have had their most exciting impact upon Christ Church. The preaching of 'new heavens, new earth' as the Christian hope, and going on to explain its practical implications for Christian mission, has resulted in a more holistic approach to mission, achieving a far greater degree of both confidence and clarity. This has been particularly true of two projects established since preaching with this emphasis began: a lunch club called Grapevine for marginalized local people which takes place on the first Sunday of every month, and participation in a night shelter run through the winter months for homeless people with other local churches.

Both projects have been consciously promoted within our congregations as providing the opportunity to be involved in 'building for the kingdom of God'. Sermons preached at the launch of Grapevine and the night shelter emphasized the role of the resurrection of Jesus in showing the breaking into the world of God's kingdom. They included explanations of 'gospel ministry' as being all those acts that, in the name of Jesus, seek to be part of seeing God's kingdom grow, from the basis established by his resurrection to the point when Jesus returns and completes this process of restoring creation. It was made clear that the building of this kingdom is God's work rather than ours; nonetheless, an emphasis was placed upon our calling to be part of this work by allowing his Spirit to work through us. This was then linked to the work of Grapevine and the night shelter and people were invited to become part of this kingdom work.

The effect of this theological emphasis has been to sweep away any uncertainty over the status of this work, enabling 'social outreach' to take its full place alongside more 'classical evangelism' as 'gospel ministry' and at the heart of the church's mission agenda. A large part of this theological confidence has been achieved through an emphasis on the eschatological truth that every piece of kingdom work built upon the foundation of Jesus will last in the future which God has promised to bring in the new heavens and new earth. Christ Church has had the tradition, like other churches, of choosing a 'motto verse' for each year to give the church purpose and direction. For 2008, 1 Corinthians 15.58 was chosen precisely to reinforce this point about the permanence of work done 'for the kingdom'. Using Paul's exhortation to the Corinthian church, I preached at the start of that year on its truth that because of Jesus' resurrection and its pledge of the certainty of God's coming new creation, we too could be certain that our 'labour in the Lord' would not be 'in vain'.[2]

Other parts of 1 Corinthians have also played a role in establishing the permanence of such 'building for the kingdom', provided that it is based upon the right foundation. An important passage here has been 1 Corinthians 3.10–14, with its warnings about 'not laying any foundation other than the one already laid, which is Jesus Christ' and making sure that any building upon this foundation is with 'gold, silver and costly stones' rather than 'wood, hay and straw'.[3] This has been used alongside Tom Wright's illustration of a master architect commissioning dozens of craftsmen to work away at features that will, one day, be somehow used to form part of the huge building he is constructing.[4] The 'somehow' element of this is significant, as it acknowledges the uncertainty on how this will precisely be the case while underlining the call to faith that Paul is making in passages like 1 Corinthians 3.

Another relevant passage that we have made use of is 1 Corinthians 13, with its emphasis upon the permanence of acts of self-giving love. Congregations sometimes have a tendency to see this passage as simply a rather poetic description of how wonderful love is, so it has come as quite a revelation to hear it used as a very practical message that all acts of self-giving love built upon the foundation of Jesus will last in the new creation.[5] The worship song 'I want to serve the purpose of God' contains the lines, 'I want to build with silver and gold in this generation', and also 'I want to give my life for something that will last forever'. This song and particularly the latter line has taken on a special significance at Christ Church as we have sought to draw out the implications of 'new heavens, new earth' for holistic mission.

This affirmation of such a holistic understanding of 'the gospel' at Christ Church has proved very significant for those whose instinctive calling has always been to care for the poor and oppressed. For many this has been extremely inspiring, particularly those who have been inclined to see themselves as 'doers' and 'carers' rather than being 'into theology'. Recognizing that what they have always believed intuitively is undergirded by a far stronger biblical theology than they previously supposed has proved extremely energizing to their ministry and this whole area of the work of the church. It has also, however, brought a greater degree of challenge because the deeper theological base for this work has then served to make it more accountable. Rather than being simply 'led by the heart', the realization has developed that the nature of our social mission at Christ Church has to be very carefully thought through and evaluated if we are to make sure that it is indeed building upon 'the foundation of Jesus Christ'.

One example of this was the decision to make Grapevine completely free rather than establish the nominal charge that had been suggested 'to make sure that it is respected'. This idea, of course, would not necessarily be transferable to all contexts. Making it at Christ Church, however, was based upon thinking about what would demonstrate the grace of Jesus Christ most strongly, to both the members of Grapevine and the rest of the church, who were asked to fund it instead. Decisions about how to respond to disputes and problems that have arisen at Grapevine and at the night shelter have also been made on a similar basis, of what will most build upon 'the foundation of Jesus Christ'. Emphasizing the priority of grace has not prevented these decisions sometimes involving quite a strong measure of 'tough love'. What it has made explicit is that every aspect of the care in both projects is being done 'in the name of Jesus Christ', and this has been the crucial factor, I believe, in creating their distinctively Christian atmosphere and many of the blessings that have come as a result.

Holistic mission and the development of personal faith

This approach has also been responsible for bringing about a measure of integration between such social mission and more classical evangelism. When Grapevine was first established in 2007, a key part of the ethos we decided upon was that it would love people for Jesus' sake rather than simply serving as a hook to preach 'the gospel' to them (understood along traditional lines). However, being freed to express this love and care with no strings attached then brought about some very natural opportunities for helpers to share their personal faith in Jesus Christ. Tom Wright has argued that evangelism flourishes best when the Church displays such advance signs of God's new creation because it is then embodying the salvation that it is offering to people.[6] When this happens it creates a context in which people genuinely want to know what is lying at the basis of what they are seeing. Wright suggests that in Jesus' case it was what he himself did to display God's salvation that gained him a willing audience to speak about it. This links to the thought of other writers like Graham Tomlin, who suggests that the primary evangelistic calling set out to Christians in the New Testament is to lead distinctive lives that 'set apart Christ as Lord' *and are then* 'prepared to give an answer for the hope that you have' (1 Peter 3.15). This passage from 1 Peter assumes that if Christians are living under the lordship of Jesus Christ, they will, sooner or later, have to answer questions from others about this. Tomlin's explanation of this is that when people experience holiness in Christians, particularly self-giving love, it will always provoke the questions that then work to make personal witness appropriate and unforced.[7]

This is certainly what we have found at Christ Church, with the more holistic theology of gospel ministry that 'new heavens, new earth' has brought enhancing rather than diluting the emphasis upon a personal sharing of faith. Much of this has occurred within the context of the pastoral ministry that has extended out of Grapevine. The emergence of particular needs, combined with the trust built up in relationships, eventually made the offer of prayer to some of its members completely appropriate. Seeking to build on this, we have established a place within the church where Grapevine members can move to after the lunch to light a candle either for themselves or for someone else and to be prayed for. The manner in which this aspect of Grapevine was established was important, with its invitation being 'light touch' and its separate location enabling members to retain their freedom on whether or not to respond. Later on, at the Christmas lunch, it then felt completely natural to ask one of the Grapevine leaders to speak for a few minutes about 'what Christmas means to me'. These very gentle and persuasive forms of evangelism proved encouragingly effective, partly because of their suitability to a 'non-book culture', but mainly because they have grown very naturally out of the guests' own response to the love that they have received. Within a couple of years of being formed, Grapevine had become a completely inclusive but distinctive Christian community 'meeting people where they are but not leaving them there'.

This strengthening of all aspects of mission through a more holistic understanding of the gospel has shown itself in other areas. As mentioned earlier, our 9.30 a.m. service at Christ Church is built around attracting newcomers to Christ Church.[8] Particularly because of its 'sssh free' nature (its complete toleration and full inclusion of children and young families) this service has attracted large numbers into a thriving new congregation. Our evangelism strategy has then been to build upon this by encouraging members of the Sssh Free Church to attend the Alpha course. For many, coming on Alpha has been crucial in the further development of their personal faith. For others, the most important factor in working towards the same outcome has been the opportunity to be involved in 'building for the kingdom' through the church's social outreach, particularly the night shelter. This work has struck a deep chord with many newcomers who are willing to take Christianity seriously if they see that it 'makes a difference'.

Having noticed this happening, I have sought to use sermons to speak into this context and give it further encouragement. With so many newcomers at the Sssh Free Church, many of the talks take an 'apologetics' approach, seeking to explain the basis of Christianity and speak into the experience members are already having through belonging to church. As part of a sermon series called 'The things Jesus came to bring us' (including such titles as 'Forgiveness' and 'Peace'), I included a talk on 'Purpose'. This talk aimed to give kingdom explanations for why those members involved in the night shelter were receiving such a buzz from being involved in this work. This, I suggested, was all part of the paradoxical kingdom truth, that we start finding 'life to the full' when we are prepared to give our lives away for Jesus and the good news of his kingdom. After that sermon a number of members of the 9.30 a.m. service signed up to help at the night shelter, giving a significant boost to both that project and the overall life of the church.

Much the same message has been delivered to the helpers at the large children's holiday club we run each year. I have sought to explain why they receive such fulfilment from devoting a week 'to be' as well as speak the good news to children. From this basis I have built more kingdom theology into the Alpha course, particularly stressing the exciting and radical invitation that Jesus makes to his followers to become part of extending his kingdom. For many of our members, this message, speaking into the experience of the kingdom of God that they are already having, has proved the critical factor in their move towards a more conscious personal faith. More than once it has caused us to reflect on the parallel to Jesus calling the disciples to 'on the job' kingdom training. Perhaps the most exciting and encouraging manifestation of this was when some members of Grapevine asked if they could help at the night shelter because they wanted to help people less fortunate than themselves.

Another related aspect of such holistic mission encouraging the growth of personal faith has been through its demonstration that Christianity is subversive rather than being oriented to the status quo. The New Malden area is largely middle class and affluent, and living within this culture can create considerable anxiety among both non-Christians and Christians as they recognize that their lifestyles are a direct cause of the world's injustice. Aware that they are caught up in powers and structures larger than themselves (sometimes described in terms like 'the rat race'), many combine a sense of helplessness about this with a genuine yearning to rebel against this 'oppression'. Included within this is the innate desire for justice that Wright argues is present within all human beings and frequently provides a surprisingly strong impulse to be part of the solution to injustice rather than its cause.[9]

It is here that the political aspects of Wright's thought have made an impact. This has been especially true in drawing out the 'principalities and powers' and modern day 'Caesars' that are dethroned by actions that proclaim that 'Jesus is Lord'.[10] Christ Church projects such as Grapevine and the night shelter, together with wider causes such as supporting Fair Trade and debt relief for the Third World, have therefore been promoted as aspects of proclaiming that 'Jesus is Lord and, therefore, the free market economy isn't!' This has created resonance in a number of our members with their yearning for justice, and has been a crucial factor in the growth of their Christian faith. Such actions have formed a vital part of demon-strating that authentic Christianity, rather than being seen as safe and 'middle class', is deeply challenging to the political and social status quo and those of us caught up in maintaining it. This in turn has encouraged a greater humility (not always present in evan-gelical churches) about how short a distance we have progressed in addressing justice issues and how much we have to learn from other churches – those of other traditions and those situated in areas where poverty is so much greater.

Proclaiming the lordship of Jesus Christ

While this holistic approach to mission at Christ Church has com-pletely reinforced the need for personal conversion, it has done so by setting it in a broader context: an understanding of the gospel as the proclamation that Jesus is Lord because, through his death and resurrection, the powers of evil have been defeated and God's new world has begun. This has enabled such biblical themes as the kingdom of God and the resurrection to have an increased prominence and ensured that preaching upon the cross has focused on the death of Jesus as God's answer to evil rather than simply 'my' personal sin.

In terms of our evangelism, proclaiming Jesus as Lord rather than simply a 'personal Saviour' has brought about not only a more holistic approach to mission but also a far greater integration of the call to live radically reshaped lives. In the suburban context of New Malden this has resulted in an approach to evangelism similar to that which Paul delivered to the pagans in Thessalonica.[11] In proclaiming the resurrection of Jesus, we have called for a turning from modern day idols, with all their dehumanizing effects, to the fully human form of living found through submitting to the lordship of Jesus Christ. This has been no easy task in an area where the size of houses, make of cars, nature of holidays and children's achievements carry major symbolism within the implicit narrative of where people's lives should be heading. The shift in approach has also not always been straightforward for some longer-term members of Christ Church, mainly because its expansion of the meaning of repentance has delivered as big a challenge to us as it has to the newcomers!

Rather than seeking the rescue of individuals for another place, Christ Church has now fully shifted its emphasis to welcome into a community that is building *now* for that future which God has initiated through the resurrection of Jesus and is committed to bringing to completion. The next chapter outlines some of the ways in which this eschatology has further changed the community into which we are seeking to welcome people.

6

Tom Wright's theology in church life

The theology of Tom Wright, most obvious in the way that it has changed our practice of mission, has made a significant impact on other aspects of our life at Christ Church, New Malden. In many cases Wright's theology has worked to supply projects and developments that already under way with a greater measure of theology, working to clarify their purpose and then increase their impact.

Welcome into a 'kingdom community' for everyone

Like many evangelical churches, Christ Church has had a tendency throughout its history to be a 'gathered' congregation, with its major emphasis on teaching 'the faithful'. Over the last decade and a half, largely initiated by my predecessor as vicar, this emphasis shifted, with Christ Church seeking to become more of a parish church and more inclusive of 'unchurched' people in the local area. This transition has not been an easy process and in the last few years it is engagement with Wright's theology that has given much greater confidence and precision to this process.

What has helped here is Wright's explanation of the eschatological basis behind the different praxis of Jesus and the Pharisees.[1] This has led us to a more determined effort to eschew a 'pre-kingdom' ecclesiology of separation from the outside world in favour of an approach reflecting the radical and life-changing inclusion that Jesus used as a sign of the arrival of God's kingdom. A major part of this has been seeking to replace the fear of 'contamination' from the outside world with the expectation that 'contamination from the church' will work the other way around. This has brought a greater confidence to engage with people in the local area and proclaim that God is now welcoming everyone, without exception, to become part of his people.

The most obvious manifestation of this, mentioned in the previous chapter, is our 9.30 a.m. service, designated as 'sssh free', and our intention to do everything possible to remove the barriers preventing newcomers, particularly young families, coming to church.[2] Once again it is the theological basis to this – that the old era of separation is over and God's kingdom is now open to everyone – that has provided the real confidence in the delivery of this welcome and its success. Like our social mission, this approach has aimed to 'meet people where they are but not leave them there'. We have therefore sought to follow up the welcome and incorporation of newcomers into the church with an appropriate programme of discipleship, including some of the factors already mentioned. The result has been a very significant growth in the amount of 'unchurched' people coming to Christ Church, many of whom express genuine surprise at the welcome they have received.

Justification and 'boundary markers'

Wright's recasting of 'justification by faith' as an ecclesiological doctrine has proved extremely helpful in responding to the issues that have emerged once newcomers have joined Christ Church. The influx of so many newcomers (in many ways rather similar to the church in the first century, when Gentiles 'swamped' the originally Jewish church) has provoked important issues surrounding their adoption, or otherwise, of traditional 'boundary markers'. The assertion of baptism and faith in Jesus the Messiah as the only badges of membership that count has been particularly important in this context, both in the full inclusion of our many children and in according an equality of status to those still 'young in the faith'.[3] This has been challenging to some of our long-term members who have sometimes wanted to retain further symbols and praxis as markers of proper membership, including, for instance, membership of a Bible Study Group, attendance at the Parish Prayer Meeting, being members of the church's system for financial giving, and even opening the church Bibles during sermons. However, actively letting go of such things as 'boundary markers' has been crucial to acknowledging the ways in which God is working in the lives of newcomers and looking for fresh ways of encouraging this. In several cases these fresh ways have involved the repackaging of very similar 'products', particularly in terms of Bible study and prayer. But the liberation of these things from having 'boundary marker' status appears to have allowed greater freedom for God's Spirit to move within them.

The challenge of this understanding of 'justification by faith' has not just come to our long-term members. Wright's explanation of the financial collection for the Jerusalem church by the Gentile churches as a practical demonstration of the doctrine of 'justification' has made us look for similar ways in which our newcomers can express their oneness with our longer-term members. One example of this was a 'Harvest Supper' at which a number of relative newcomers to our 9.30 a.m. service worked hard to provide an evening of food and entertainment mainly aimed at our longer-term members. Drawing on Wright's exposition of Romans, such events have been explained as having two aims: providing practical opportunities for our 'Gentiles' to express their gratitude to the 'Jews' for preserving the inheritance they are now receiving, and giving our 'Jews' a tangible demonstration of the rich blessing that God always intended to bring to his people through the incorporation of such 'Gentile' newcomers.[4]

Understanding 'justification' as an ecclesiological and indeed ecumenical truth has also influenced our relationship with other churches in the local area.[5] It is often assumed that doctrine needs to be downplayed in order to move towards greater Christian unity. In our case, reflection upon the doctrine of 'justification by faith' has led us towards a greater determination to build really good and meaningful relationships with these churches. Promoted on the basis of rejecting any boundary markers other than baptism and the profession of faith in Jesus Christ, this 'ecumenical doctrine' has particularly given greater energy and resolve to our partnership in the gospel with other churches. This showed itself in the ecumenical nature of the night shelter, which we specifically promoted as an opportunity to express our 'oneness' with all those others proclaiming that Jesus is Lord. It has given further stimulation to existing ecumenical partnerships such as Oxygen, a major youth project established by Christ Church and other local churches some years before. Such projects often respond to areas of really desperate need, and we have seen something of the power that is unleashed through the unity of the church proclaiming to the dividing principalities and powers that 'their time is up'.[6]

Justification and fellowship

Reflection upon the importance of giving meaningful and practical expression to the doctrine of 'justification by faith' has led us towards the active promotion of fellowship at Christ Church. From being regarded as essentially light relief from the more central elements of 'worship', church socials and parties now have a far more overt theological significance. Central to this was the establishment in 2004 of the FUN (standing for Friendship Unlimited Now) Committee, or FUNC, at Christ Church. Despite its frivolous sounding title, the aim behind the formation of this group was the very serious one of building a greater depth of community and relationship across Christ Church. Wright's work on 'justification' makes it clear that the doctrine was formed out of the very practical issue of whom one can sit at the same table with as a fellow Christian brother or sister.[7] In a direct response to this, the work of FUNC has largely concentrated on the encouragement of our unity through the provision of further opportunities for members of the church to eat, share time and celebrate together. It has often been encounter with the warmth and seriousness of this fellowship, accompanied by an explanation of its theological significance within sermons, that has been the vital factor in retaining newcomers within the church.

A significant episode that put this principle to the test was when we took the decision to incorporate members of Grapevine within the annual FUNC trip to the coast at Littlehampton. This decision caused considerable anxiety among some members of Christ Church honest enough to admit their concern at being with people 'not like us'. The theological response to this issue was crucial: the issue of whether or not to incorporate Grapevine members presented a vital test of our Christian belief. Parallels were made with the Antioch incident in Galatians 2 when Paul opposed Peter for withdrawing from eating with Gentile believers, and the idea was put forward that the united nature of the Littlehampton trip would form a decisive demonstration of our belief in 'justification by faith'. The trip went ahead, with over a hundred people from widely different social backgrounds travelling, eating and having fun together; it proved a wonderful experience and a crucial demonstration to everyone involved of the radical distinctiveness of our Christian faith.

Creation, idolatry and dualism

A related aspect of the impact of Tom Wright's theology upon Christ Church has been in its encouragement of a much more positive theology of creation. Throughout much of its history, Christ Church has tended to maintain something of a distance from the world and particularly its forms of entertainment and enjoyment. The most obvious manifestation of this was a ban on alcohol on the premises (other than at Holy Communion!) which lasted from 1866 through to 2009. This separation of church from 'the things of the world', however, often seemed to have the effect of encouraging a greater degree of secularism, since the use of these things by members outside of church was then removed from having any Christian direction or input.

Wright's theology has made a difference here in his insistence on the goodness of God's creation and the equal dangers of idolatry and 'dualism'.[8] Responding to idolatry, as mentioned already, is a major issue in New Malden and Wright's theology has been very helpful here. Using the definition of idolatry as 'treating created things as if they are God', sermons at Christ Church have tried to show the dehumanization that occurs once we 'worship' things as diverse as work, friendships, food and drink, by placing them at the centre of our lives. These talks have tried to show the practical outworking of Wright's explanation of the spiritual forces that are activated once this happens. These include such idols then demanding 'sacrifices' from the other good things in our lives and ultimately failing to deliver on what they have promised anyway.[9]

Wright's warnings about the spiritual law of worship – that we become more like what we worship and therefore steadily less 'human' when we worship idols – has also been helpful in spelling out the dangers here.[10] In a setting where enormous pressure exists to make life essentially about the accumulation of wealth, possessions and achievement, giving practical examples of the 'deception' involved in such 'idolatry', and being frank about its dehumanizing effects, has become a very important part of trying to combat it.

It has been just as significant to emphasize that avoidance of idolatry should not lead to 'dualism': in other words, a denial of the goodness of God's creation. Here Wright's further definition of idolatry as 'treating something *good* as if it were God' has given us greater precision over the problem.[11] This has led to a major emphasis at Christ Church upon avoiding idolatry *by using God's creation wisely and well*, rather than not using it at all. There are obviously some exceptions to this, such as the need to abstain, permanently or temporarily, from things like alcohol if they have been a particular problem. Overall, however, our reflections upon creation, idolatry and dualism have produced a strong emphasis upon enjoying 'the good things of creation' to the full, through giving them their proper place, *below God*, as things made by him to enrich our lives.

This has become the other vital strand of the work of FUNC, which seeks to demonstrate the fullness of life that comes from such an approach. Musical sing-alongs, film nights, tenpin bowling trips, quiz nights and barn dances – all take place regularly at Christ Church as a result of this determination to see our proper use and enjoyment of God's good creation as a core part of our worship through its anticipation of the new creation. The decision to repeal the long-standing ban on the consumption of alcoholic drinks, subject to a number of safeguards to protect against misuse and those vulnerable to this, was recognized as an important part of upholding our rejection of dualism along with idolatry.

Another consequence of this has been the active encouragement of a number of talented musicians and poets within Christ Church to express their gifts in concerts held on Sunday afternoons. This has worked towards the aim of more actively encouraging that creation of beauty that Wright sees as central to the Church's anticipation of new creation.[12] It has also served to give a much deeper affirmation within Christ Church of those for whom this quest for beauty particularly resonates. Once again, the confident integration of 'real life' with church and the healthy attitude displayed towards enjoying 'life to the full' has been deeply attractive to our newcomers, causing them to ask what lies at its heart.

In response to this, I have particularly sought to devise sermon series within our services in order to give further explanation to this. One series was called 'What's so God-given about . . . ?', and its various talks focused upon food and drink, friendships, parties, music, sport and sex. The temptation to focus these talks upon negatives was resisted; instead they aimed to be wholly positive, concentrating on the goodness and God-given nature of the subject and, from this basis, setting out an exciting vision for their best possible use. Other sermon series have sought to further encourage this integration; another, with the title 'Being a Christian . . .', in successive weeks dealt with '. . . in the workplace', '. . . in front of the TV', '. . . in the kitchen' (chiefly on Fair Trade issues), '. . . in the dining room' (on hospitality), and '. . . in the bedroom' (once again on sex). The content of these was met with surprise by some congregation members who were used to sermons being about more 'spiritual matters'. In most quarters, however, this feeling was swiftly replaced with considerable relief that the Bible contained so much that could speak to all these areas of everyday life. Together with the work of FUNC and the invitation to be involved in the mission of the church, this approach has been crucial to presenting Christianity as the path to that fully human way of living to which Jesus came to restore us.

Another aspect of this challenge has been a greater focus upon the Trinity. As happens in many churches, members of Christ Church have tended to view the Trinity as an important but rather abstract piece of doctrine. Following Wright's lead, we have increasingly recognized and sought to present the deeply practical nature of the doctrine of the Trinity and its vital role in helping us to avoid idolatry and dualism.[13] Sermons on the Trinity have sought to show the relationship between monotheism and the rejection of idolatry, before proceeding to unpack how creational, covenantal and Trinitarian monotheism helps us to avoid dualism. One sermon series for our more established congregation was called 'Jargon-busting the Trinity', and looked at a different Trinitarian term each week, seeking to explain what this term was trying to safeguard about our understanding of God and his relationship to the world: titles included 'Homoousios – spin or substance?' and 'Perichoresis – dancing around a difficult subject'. While the exploration of such terms might seem unnecessary and needlessly complex, we made a disciplined effort each week to stick to one piece of 'Trinitarian jargon' and lay the major emphasis upon the practical difference it made to Christian living. This idea could have been off-putting, but the result was that members of Christ Church felt a sense of empowerment as they recognized the practical relevance of a doctrine that they not previously realized was meant to function in that way.

An interesting side-effect of this focus upon the Trinity and its practical relevance has been a greater understanding of the distinctiveness of Christianity from other religions. In many parts of the western world there is anxiety about the increasing rise of Islam, and New Malden is no exception. The way we respond to this fear and its various manifestations obviously requires a good deal of care to ensure that we are combating rather than fostering prejudice. The reflections upon the Trinity reported above have helped by enabling us to have respect for Islam's strong and effective desire to repudiate idolatry, at the same time maintaining our belief that such repudiation does not necessarily lead to the Muslim idea that God cannot therefore be personally known and intimately involved in the world. This deeper understanding of the distinctive nature of Jewish/Christian monotheism, together with greater confidence about the sense that the Incarnation makes within it, has led to a fruitful and constructive dialogue with Muslims in our area. Discussions with both Muslim students and a local imam have taken place, and I was asked to speak at an interfaith event to mark the anniversary of the 7/7 London bombings. In all these settings I found that a greater understanding of the differences between Christian and Muslim monotheism and careful reflection upon the factors that have led to this have produced an informed engagement and much better relationship.

The development of Christian character

Throughout these developments, encouraging our members into a deeper relationship with God has remained central to Christ Church. In fact, as new people have come into the church, the yearning for 'spirituality' that Wright identifies as intrinsic within people has been particularly apparent.[14] We have especially noticed this when people have become parents for the first time; they often appear to be searching very obviously for something to speak into the 'God-moment' they experienced when their child was born.[15] The whole nature of our Sssh Free Church at 9.30 a.m. and its integration with the Alpha course has been an attempt to respond to this reaching out for God and then to encourage its path to a growing relationship with him through Jesus Christ.[16]

It is here that Wright's thought on the development of Christian virtue or character has been particularly helpful in clarifying what needs to happen 'after you believe'. With its strong emphasis on salvation coming as a gift, Christ Church, like many evangelical churches, has sometimes appeared a little uncertain about how much to stress a sustained effort to lead holy lives. More than once, for instance, I have heard people using the phrase 'let go and let God' or warning against the dangers of 'striving' or 'letting works in through the back door'. The implication has been that making too much of an effort to lead holy lives might somehow form a denial of the need for God's grace and the work of his Spirit. In addressing this, we have begun to emphasize that Spirit-filled and grace-driven living is precisely about the concentrated effort to work hard to anticipate the destiny that we will possess in the new creation.[17] Sermons, both thematic and expository, have played an important role in this, setting out a vision of God's ultimate intention for our future and giving practical examples of the habit-forming decisions we need to be taking now to start being transformed by the Spirit into the person that God will confirm us to be in the new creation. In an era where gyms and fitness centres are ever more popular, the effort to become physically fit has provided a helpful illustration of the way in which taking decisions that might feel unnatural at first can eventually become habitual and in turn transforming, as more of our future destiny becomes evident in the present.[18]

This sort of illustration is also helpful in its connection with the resurrection emphasis upon the vital importance of our bodies. 1 Corinthians is often viewed as a fairly disparate letter with Paul trawling though a number of varied subjects before finally, in chapter 15, focusing on another one, the resurrection. In contrast to this, Wright has shown how every section within 1 Corinthians presents the difference that the resurrection can and should make to both church life and personal ethics.[19] In terms of sexual ethics, this has resulted in an emphasis on the truth that, because of their future resurrection in the new creation, what we do with our bodies in the present really matters. A really positive emphasis upon the goodness of sex has combined with a clear message from 1 Corinthians 6 about the need for the use of our bodies, and the integration of this with developing more godly minds forming an anticipation of their future role in worshipping God in the new creation.

The encouragement of forgiveness

Forgiveness is another important area where this emphasis on 'new creation theology' has impacted upon us at Christ Church. Forgiveness is a subject that is often difficult to handle at church, particularly when ministering to people who have suffered particularly badly at the hands of others. Any simple insistence that people need to forgive those who have hurt them in order to be forgiven by God can seem unbearably trite and cause immense damage. Here Wright's work on evil has been helpful, in the first place through encouraging the acknowledgement of its full reality.[20] Use of the Psalms, much advocated by Wright, particularly promotes the naming of evil and vocalizing of anger at its effects, both of which have great pastoral significance.[21] Equally important has been presenting Jesus' death as the execution of God's judgement upon this evil. Following on from this we have sought to indicate how a vital aspect of our resulting release from evil in the new creation will be our liberation from the dehumanizing effect of our anger with those responsible for inflicting this. This has helped to explain why seeking to forgive others in the present is an important part of our calling to live lives that anticipate that future when sin and evil will have no more dominion over us.[22]

Existing pastoral psychology and practice has thus been supplied with an increased amount of theological foundation. Giving greater theological explanation of this through sermons, however, has nonetheless brought a good deal of help to those previously perplexed at forgiveness being 'required' from them. Illustrations from the remarkable 'truth and reconciliation' process in post-apartheid South Africa have been used to portray forgiveness as less to do with duty, and more about allowing God's Spirit to lead us further towards our destiny in the new creation. This has enabled us to 'start from where people are', suggesting that often simply reaching the point of *wanting* to forgive those who have hurt us is a major step towards this future. From the basis of this encouragement and the all-important acknowledgement of evil that accompanied it, we have seen people make remarkable progress towards being able to show a full forgiveness, even when the hurt that they have received has been considerable.

The encouragement of the use of gifts and talents

Another aspect of life at Christ Church that we have particularly encouraged in recent times is 'every member ministry'. Central to this was the establishment of the G&T Committee (concerned with 'gifts and talents' rather than 'gin and tonic'!) to oversee the identification and deployment of the gifts and talents of the members of our congregations. Rather than approach this in terms of finding people to do particular jobs, we have tried instead to let the gifts and talents that God has given to our members set the agenda for some of what the church is doing. A questionnaire was used to establish what talents members of the congregation have to offer, and then we sought to reflect and pray upon where God is calling these gifts to be deployed.

Once again, Wright's theology has given precision and clarity to this process, particularly through his emphasis upon the church anticipating its role as 'priests and rulers' in the new creation.[23] We lay a particular stress on the unique nature of the gifts that God has given to each of us and the way in which, when we use these gifts to serve him and others, we start becoming more fully the person he made us to be. As mentioned already, we have seen people particularly flourishing through their role in the developing social mission of Christ Church. Following on from this, we have encouraged the similar growth of others through their use of talents as diverse as gardening, administration, music and driving. Encouraging the use of our gifts to serve others, both within Christ Church and in life outside the church, has become a vital part of displaying that fully human form of living that we are promised in the new creation and which starts to become available to us once we are following Jesus Christ.

This has led to a further appreciation of the role of *encouragement* itself as a spiritual gift. Already valued for the difference it made to church life, we have started to recognize the prophetic nature of encouragement, with some being particularly gifted not only in recognizing the person God has made others to be but also in being supplied with the words to express and confirm this. These 'words', through their engendering of 'courage' often at a time when someone has started exercising their gifts in a new area of church life, have made an immense difference. Previously seen as something merely rather 'nice', we have begun to see the vital and spiritual role of encouragement in working to bring more of the reality of God's future new creation into the present reality of our lives, both as individuals and as a church.

Church services

The result of all this has been an emphasis upon church services at Christ Church that seek to celebrate and reflect God's new creation and, from this basis, inform and guide the role that we are called to play in 'building for the kingdom'. Services are therefore presented as key focal moments, shaping and nourishing our collective and personal worship of God throughout the week within the various locations that he has placed us.

The Bible and preaching have remained central to these services. Wright's emphasis upon the Bible as foundational for calling Christians to live within its story of God's redemption of the cosmos has led him to stress the value of the public reading of Scripture and also the use of the lectionary (an authorized list of appointed Scripture readings) to ensure an even coverage of its contents.[24] He similarly advocates the use of liturgy (set forms and structures of worship) and regularly reciting the creeds during church services.[25] Reflecting the 'new creation' principle of time, space and matter being good things that the Church should reclaim rather than abandon, Wright emphasizes the value of observing the Christian year and protecting the historic buildings of the church as part of safeguarding and expressing these truths.[26]

In terms of our more traditional services most of these principles are very obviously upheld, using the rationale that Wright has offered for their basis to give greater confidence to their delivery.

An important exception here is the use of the sermon series that Christ Church has traditionally preferred to the lectionary. As mentioned earlier, a number of *topical* sermon series have been given at Christ Church. Most of our series, however, particularly within our more traditional services at 8 a.m. and 11 a.m., have tended to work through biblical books over periods of one or two months. A greater depth of focus has been achieved in these series than is allowed by the lectionary; nonetheless they have still sought to reflect the Christian year and ensure an even coverage of the Bible's contents.

Reflecting the post-Christendom context in which the UK is now located, things are rather different in our less traditional services at 9.30 a.m. and 6.30 p.m. As mentioned already, the 9.30 a.m. is essentially a mission service with a priority upon being as accessible as possible to children and newcomers. This context, together with an acknowledgement of the generally low level of biblical literacy now apparent within the UK population, has led us to compromise on our application of some of the principles set out above. Short Bible readings are preferred to longer ones and both liturgy and creeds are used sparingly. In their place, thematic and expository sermons give regular coverage of the broad sweep of the Bible's story, often making use of pictures, summaries and headings conveyed through the multi-media equipment we employ within these services. In recognition of the need to start a lot 'further back' and build, rather than assume a Christian understanding, many of these sermons seek to engage with the most pressing questions and issues that newcomers to the church are currently facing, before attempting to show how God is calling us to understand and respond to these issues in the light of the biblical story of salvation and new creation.

Even in our ministry to those who have been Christians for longer, we recognize the need to acknowledge rather than ignore the cultural context in which many people's assumptions and attitudes are located. This is particularly evident within our 6.30 p.m. service, where some elements reflect the increasingly postmodern cultural context and others seek to challenge the world-view underlying this. Tom Wright has expressed concerns about the postmodern nature of the recent 'worship song' approach, where the narrative of God's saving actions (present within many older hymns) is often replaced by a pastiche of Christian images selected by their ability to create resonance.[27] The power of such songs to connect with people is undeniable, however, and they powerfully express our calling to reflect creation's praise to God; this has led us to adopt this style of sung worship at our 6.30 p.m. service, set within an equally postmodern 'café style' layout. These concessions to postmodernism, however, have been balanced by an approach that seeks to avoid the songs chosen becoming too individualistic and retains a clear structure and direction for the service. The sermons at 6.30 p.m. make plentiful use of pictures and images in their effort to engage a postmodern congregation while also seeking to confront the world-view and praxis of this culture, and explain the challenge issued to it by the story of Scripture. Included within these sermons, and very much inspired by Wright's theology, have been efforts to challenge tendencies within this congregation towards modern forms of Gnosticism. One example of this was a sermon series that asked, over successive weeks, 'Why *on earth* do we need . . . the Old Testament?', '. . . the Church?' and '. . . the Sacraments?'.

As a reflection of this desire to express a fuller theology of new creation, sacramental worship has grown in importance at Christ Church. Baptism is now recognized as a very special moment, at which our congregations witness God's new creation breaking into the old. Our desire to keep this sacred moment alive in the consciousness of those being baptized has led us to film our many baptisms and to present a DVD to the child or adult, with the aim that this will facilitate their living out a baptized life.[28] In terms of both baptism and Holy Communion, Wright's theology has begun to influence our progress towards a greater engagement with movement and ritual. Acknowledging that we are in much greater danger of falling into a dualistic rejection of creation than into idolatry, we are seeking to replace a fear of sacramental worship with an excitement about its vital role in displaying and bringing the coming of God's kingdom 'on earth as in heaven'. The implementation of this is still at a relatively early stage; our aim is to explore all the ways in which such sacramental worship can bring the richness and colour of God's new creation into our worship and how this can nourish us for mission.

The encouragement of the full ministry of women

A central aspect of the development of Christ Church in recent times has been a very strong emphasis on the full ministry of women. There are, of course, major differences on this issue within evangelicalism, and most of the relevant textual and theological arguments lie beyond the scope of this book. However, in two particular areas the theology of Tom Wright has played a very crucial role here. The first is in the context of the Gospel resurrection narratives, where Wright draws attention to the fact that it was the women to whom Jesus entrusted the message that he had risen. This radical transformation of the previous all-male apostolate on the very first day of the new creation is presented in John 20. Peter and the other male apostles need, in John 21, to be rehabilitated before they can take up their responsibilities, while Mary Magdalene is given her commission straight away.[29] Going back to the original goodness of creation, Wright also stresses the importance of the man and the woman reflecting in their unity the image of God as they are given stewardship over the earth. Fractured through 'the fall', the re-establishment of this 'image-bearing unity' through the full role of women's leadership, alongside that of men, is therefore a central aspect of the coming of God's new creation, which the Church is called to reflect in its role as 'priests and rulers'.[30]

Encouraged by this, Christ Church has sought to anticipate this reunification in our worship, working towards the aim of having all our services either led by a woman with a man preaching, or vice versa. This has brought about an immediate sense of increased richness, chiefly through congregations experiencing that complementary range of male and female styles and voices, in anticipation of the exciting and productive unity that God is working to restore us to in the new creation. Decision-making, pastoral care and the whole atmosphere of Christ Church have been greatly enriched by their greater reflection of that restoration of the 'divine image-bearing unity' of male and female. Reflection on this has led us to seek to have a woman and a man as our two churchwardens (the officials elected by congregations in the Church of England to work with the vicar and take particular responsibility for the fabric and finance of the church). In recent times there has been a proper concern, particularly within the evangelical tradition, about how alienating much of church culture can be to men and how this needs to be addressed.[31] The development of women's ministry has been seen by some as contributing to an 'over-feminization' of the Church, which is likely to continue this trend. At Christ Church, however, we have generally seen the very opposite, with the encouragement of the full ministry of women bringing plenty of men, as well as women, to appreciate the much greater richness that has come to the church as a result.

Responding to homosexuality

The changes in perspective reported in this book have not led Christ Church to a revisionist position on homosexual practice. Some readers will be relieved by this and others disappointed. The affirmation of women's full ministry is often presented, by both its proponents and detractors, as something that will then lead the Church further in this direction.[32] However, reflection on the male and female, together and united, representing the image of God, has if anything strengthened my conviction that a move towards an endorsement of homosexual and lesbian practice would not be right. This might appear inconsistent with principles outlined earlier that spoke of the removal of any boundary markers for the church other than baptism and faith in Jesus, and these principles have indeed strongly influenced our emphasis upon a full welcome to everyone, including those who are gay, to Christ Church. Wright's equal stress on Jesus 'meeting people where they are but not leaving them there', however, has helped us clarify an approach that seeks to combine welcome and inclusion with the belief that it is God's will for those who are homosexual to be celibate.[33]

This is by no means a universal belief among all members of Christ Church; some are perplexed about whether such a welcome can ever be genuine if it excludes an acceptance of that which people see as vital to their identity. We are clearly at a very early stage of working out how a new creation theology should show itself in our pastoral response to those who are gay. Further prayer, listening and discussion are needed here. For the moment we have arrived at an overall emphasis that sees our primary role being to welcome everyone and to combine honesty and clarity about the church's perspective on homosexual practice with a firm belief that it is the role of the Holy Spirit to change people's lives, with a priority list that is probably very different from ours. This is the present shape of our response to homosexuality – to some impossibly liberal and to others impossibly conservative – that seeks to reflect both grace and truth.

Work in progress

The reason why so much detail from the life Christ Church, New Malden is outlined here is to illustrate the difference that the theology of Tom Wright can make when it is put into practice. One positive aspect of postmodernism is that Christians today are less prepared to accept theology without seeing or hearing accounts of what the changes related to this theology will look like on the ground. In concluding this section of the book and its focus upon stories from Christ Church, some further comments are needed.

The first is to make it clear that Christ Church is far from the finished product. While the church has made significant advances in recent times, we are very aware of certain areas in which we need to become more effective. One of these is in our ministry to those of other races, particularly the many Koreans who live in New Malden. A good number of Koreans do attend Christ Church, but we know that we need to become much more integrated if we are to display the radical unity we have in Christ and, through this, challenge the dividing 'principalities and powers' present in New Malden. The further development of our sacramental worship could also clearly benefit from the creation of greater space for stillness before God in our services – not a strength of the current vicar!

Another important point is that Tom Wright has not been the only theological influence upon the church. Walter Brueggemann, Richard Bauckham, John Goldingay and Paula Gooder, alongside other biblical scholars, have been influential. As already mentioned, Graham Tomlin's thought on evangelism has been very helpful in changing our thinking and approach. The influence of Tom Wright has also had its limits. One brave member of the congregation asked me (as we overlooked Nazareth!) what parts of Wright's thought I disagreed with. There are not many things, but my answer does include my continuing belief in annihilation in terms of the fate of the lost, rather than following Wright's belief in a continuing existence alongside the loss of any remaining 'image of God'.[34] In addition, I also believe, against Wright, that rather than the husband 'taking the lead' over his wife, the New Testament points to a completely shared and mutual approach to decision-making within marriage.[35] On this basis, I encourage couples getting married at Christ Church to use the same vows as each other and discourage the bride from promising to obey her husband. As suggested by some of the things already said about church services, I also tend towards the view that the missionary context in which the Church now finds itself in the UK requires it to be far more radically reshaped than Wright is perhaps prepared to envisage.[36] While not disagreeing with the *principles* behind Wright's keenness to maintain the Church's use of liturgy, creeds, vestments and historic buildings, my own view is that a much greater priority needs to be placed upon developing radically new forms of worship to express the theological truths that Wright is seeking to uphold. In particular, I would argue that attempts to make worship more accessible and less formal are precisely what we need to do if we are to 'meet people where they are but not leave them there'.[37] Far too much traditional church in the UK is currently taking place in impressive but increasingly empty buildings, with leaders either unwilling or unable to ask the tough questions about why this might be the case. Talk of developing a 'mixed economy' of traditional worship alongside 'fresh expressions of church' can often seem more committed to preserving the former than developing the latter.

A final point needs to be made about conflict. The accounts in this book would be neither honest nor complete without an acknowledgement that some members at Christ Church have found the emphasis upon Tom Wright's theology extremely problematic. With the church having possessed such a conservative evangelical past, several have found any questioning of this tradition disturbing. This has particularly applied to suggestions that our understanding of the atonement, sin and 'the gospel' needs to become more biblical. A 'new heavens, new earth' eschatology has caused upset, especially once it started changing the church's mission agenda. Discernment has therefore been needed over the amount of 'newer theology' with which some more traditional members and congregations should be challenged. But the principle of constantly seeking to be reformed by Scripture has remained our conviction, and the church as a whole has been pushed on in this agenda and received immense blessings as a result.

7

The challenge of Tom Wright to the Church

————•◆•————

The aim of this book has been to encourage a greater engagement with Tom Wright's theology. Much of its challenge has, reflecting my own background, been obviously directed towards evangelicalism in the UK. As mentioned earlier, something of a crisis of confidence exists within a great deal of western evangelicalism, with many who have previously existed in this tradition now being inclined to doubt its ability to address the most pressing issues currently faced by the Church and society. More than in any other area, this applies to the relevance of Christianity to issues of poverty and injustice in the world and our growing awareness of the complexities behind their causation and maintenance. It is here that evangelicals need to repent of our complacency over the overwhelmingly affluent nature of the movement, and with humility search the Scriptures to locate the biblical theology that will challenge us to begin to be part of the solution to poverty and injustice rather than part of the problem.

Vital to this process is our need to acknowledge that there are major weaknesses in areas of theology traditionally regarded as evangelical strengths, namely our understanding of the Christian hope, sin, the atonement, mission and the nature and authority of the Bible. In none of these areas will it do to claim that there is 'no case to answer' and simply reassert traditional evangelical formulations. The challenge we face and our way of being truly faithful to our Reformation heritage is to revisit the Scriptures to review our doctrine and practice, knowing that there will always be vital insights there that we have missed and that are needed to augment, and in some cases replace, our existing understanding. One most challenging but important question to which we need to have an answer is, what fresh insights from the Bible have really changed our evangelical tradition in the last ten years? It is not a bad idea to ask this question in terms of our personal Christian lives as well! If we struggle to find an answer, or resent the question being asked, the chances are that our authority is resting somewhere other than the Bible. The chances are, as well, that we have long since ceased being truly relevant to the needs of those to whom we are called to minister and the most pressing issues of our culture and society. Tom Wright has declared that rather than giving first-century answers to twenty-first-century questions, the Church has often got stuck giving nineteenth-century answers to sixteenth-century questions![1] Evangelicalism needs to recognize not only the rebuke here but the challenge to have the confidence to accept that there are truths within the Bible that we have previously missed and that hold the answers to even the most difficult questions and issues faced today. Obviously it is not enough to stop there. We must then seek ways of putting these answers into practice, and this is part of the reason this book has been written in the way that it has.

This was the spirit that evangelicals within the Church of England showed around the time of the first three NEACs in 1967, 1977 and 1988. Having come out of the 'ghetto' in which evangelicalism had previously existed, the movement showed a real determination to address its weaknesses in order to be reformed for the sake of the mission to which God had called us.[2] This was typified by John Stott's comment that he preferred the title 'radical-conservative evangelical' to one simply expressing conservatism.[3] During the 1990s, however, much of evangelical Anglicanism began to lose this spirit of optimism and adventure. Wonderful developments were still happening within evangelicalism during that decade, most obviously the incredible impact of the Alpha course and then the start of the 'mission-shaped Church' movement. But in *theological* terms evangelicalism, certainly at a grassroots level, started to lose much of its confidence to address, with any freshness, the pressing issues for mission emerging during that decade. A number of factors could be seen as having brought this about. One was 'the Keele generation' growing older and their successors seeing less urgency in this agenda. Another was the continuing growth of the charismatic strand of evangelicalism, where much of the energy for change became heavily, if productively, focused on the renewal of 'worship' and 'spiritual gifts'. Of greater significance than either of these was the considerable anxiety created by the ordination of women and the rising profile of the issue of homosexuality. This, in particular, resulted in the development of a much more defensive mentality within significant sections of evangelicalism and a reduced willingness to acknowledge, let alone respond to, areas of weakness within traditional evangelicalism.[4]

Partly as a result of this, the 1990s saw the marked development of what gradually became known as 'post-evangelicalism', with increasing numbers of those who had been nurtured within the evangelical tradition becoming disillusioned as to whether the tradition held the answers to the most pressing issues facing the Church and society.[5] Such developments were not only apparent within the Church of England; significant sections of the non-conformist and house/new church movements experienced this as well. Much of the more recent 'emerging church' movement has also shown a desire to move beyond an evangelicalism that it has been tempted to view as rather tired and sterile.

Similar developments have been apparent in the USA during this same period with an increasingly conservative and reactionary evangelicalism creating a similar response. Much of this has been provoked by the apparent indifference of some American evangelicals towards economic and social injustice, compared to issues such as abortion and homosexuality. In more recent times this has been exacerbated by the seemingly uncritical support extended by many American evangelicals towards their government's foreign policy, especially following the terrorist attacks on September 11, 2001. Jim Wallis, Tony Campolo, Stanley Grenz and more recently Brian McLaren and Rob Bell are examples of leaders who have sought to resist this conservative drift and offer a fresh and positive vision for the renewal of evangelicalism. In the UK it was a very similar vision that led a group of evangelicals, including Tom Wright, in 2003 to form Fulcrum, with its aim of 'renewing the evangelical centre of the Church of England'.[6] A similar group in the USA, called Covenant, was formed in 2008. These movements have resulted in many people becoming energized and motivated about being part of a renewal of evangelicalism and, through this, seeing the further renewal of the Church.[7] In both the UK and USA, however, plenty of other Christians are moving instead to the two extremes either side of this: a conservative evangelicalism that sees the answer lying in further retrenchment, or a 'post-evangelicalism' increasingly tempted to see the whole tradition as being rather washed up and moribund.

This book has been written partly to give further encouragement to the response that avoids both of these extremes, and to do so by indicating how much exciting and dynamic biblical theology has been produced in recent times, particularly by Tom Wright but also by others, that can facilitate and inform such a positive response. The major issue facing evangelicals, if this is going to happen, is the overcoming of fear. At the national launch of Fulcrum in November 2003, Tom Wright spoke, using Ephesians 3, of the need to engage with the cosmic scope of the gospel; he also referred to Joshua 1 to indicate the courage necessary for entering this new 'territory'.[8] Speaking in Clapham, the place in London from which William Wilberforce launched his campaign to end the slave trade, Wright argued that it was a greater acknowledgement of the scope of God's plan that would bring such courage. Many Christians, he suggested, including evangelicals, were living in one or two rather scruffy rooms of a house whose other rooms, full of beautiful furniture, art treasures and libraries, remained locked and forgotten. Wright's call was that it was therefore time 'to open the locked doors and explore all the treasures of the gospel, especially those to which Scripture itself points but our traditions, not least our evangelical traditions, have screened out'.

This would involve, Wright declared, having the courage to seek to bring God's order, justice and wise stewardship to the whole of his creation, and to resist the dualist fears that suggest that such an agenda is either 'unspiritual' or pointless; this would be not as a second order action or as an 'implication of the gospel', but as part of the gospel itself. This rejection of dualism would further involve, Wright added, the development of a properly biblical sacramental theology and challenging the fear that this would automatically lead to idolatry or crypto-paganism. Much of evangelicalism, he suggested, 'had been so anxious about the greenfly on the roses it had decided to pave over the garden with concrete!' Finally, Wright highlighted the courage needed to give a full commitment to the Church in its God-given unity in diversity. While acknowledging the vital role of holy living and the necessity of opposition and disagreement, Wright called for a theology of church that would resist the fear that drives people to create structures to make themselves feel safe and superior to other Christians.[9]

Such a vision for Fulcrum, Wright declared, would work not only towards the renewal of evangelical Anglicanism but towards the renewal of the Anglican Church itself. Echoing, in many ways, the call made at Keele 36 years before, Wright said that the launch of Fulcrum represented 'a call to evangelical Anglicans of whatever background to grow up, to work together, to play a full part in the Church of England and the wider Anglican Communion, to make the running instead of always reacting, to be in the front row of innovative gospel-work, to hold together what Wilberforce and others held together, to oppose (to be sure) the many things that must be resisted but to do so in the right spirit and always with Ephesians 3.10 as our motto and rubric'.[10] The motivation behind the writing of this book has largely been to stimulate this courage among evangelical Christians and to point to the considerable riches that become available once we take the decision to resist our fears, ask the tough questions that need to be put to our tradition, and then look to bring our Christian faith into areas that we have previously left unexplored.

My personal belief is that a great deal of this can be achieved by paying careful attention to the way in which Tom Wright has responded to challenges made to both orthodox doctrine and evangelical interpretations of the Bible. As mentioned already, evangelical responses to these issues have often been defensive, with even the best and most gracious examples usually struggling somewhat to acknowledge the validity of liberal questions and their problems with orthodoxy.[11] Wright's work has, by contrast, been markedly different, showing the ability to engage with the weaknesses within established 'orthodoxy' to which such criticism has been pointing. The result, in diverse areas that range from E. P. Sanders' work on Paul to postmodern readings of Scripture, has been to combine an examination of the areas of inadequacy within such alternative proposals with an acknowledgement of the validity of the questions and data prompting them.[12] This approach has contributed to some of the most exciting fresh insights that Wright has rediscovered in the Bible, which need to take their place within a new understanding of biblical orthodoxy. Much the same attitude has been demonstrated in the work of scholars such as John Goldingay and Richard Bauckham.

Once again, the critical issues here are to do with fear and ecclesiology. Evangelicals should avoid assuming that those raising searching questions about orthodoxy or established interpretations of the Bible are simply being destructive or even plain wicked. They need to respond to the questions and problems of fellow Christians open to the idea that something valid and important is always being raised and needs to be addressed rather than ignored. This will lead not only to much better and productive relationships with Christians of other traditions, but to a far greater chance of evangelicalism being constantly renewed in the light of fresh insights from the Bible that such conversations and dialogue will always produce.[13]

A further hope is that engagement with Tom Wright's theology will be of considerable help and inspiration to other traditions beyond that of evangelicalism. Within the Church of England and Anglican Communion, the more catholic and liberal traditions have often given greatest value to those aspects of worship and mission of the Church that Wright has sought to promote. The biblical foundations that Wright has advanced for both sacramental worship and the Church being at the forefront of promoting social justice, will, it is hoped, be welcomed with enthusiasm by catholics and liberals. In response to this, Christians from within these traditions might then be given courage to engage more deeply with some of the traditional emphases of evangelicalism, resisting their particular fears of what such an engagement might lead to. This two-way process has the potential to lead to the breaking down of some of the disastrous dichotomies that have existed for too long within the Christian Church: the divides that exist between, for example, classical evangelism and social mission, preaching and sacramental worship, the need for personal conversion and a 'high' view of the Church, 'inclusion' and 'transformation', the supremacy of grace and the need for an active pursuit of holiness. Wright's theology has provided such a strong model for integrating these different aspects of Christian belief and practice that this, as much as his understanding of 'justification by faith', has huge potential for bringing evangelicals, liberals and catholics closer together.

This applies more than anywhere else in terms of holistic mission. The utterly clear biblical foundation established for this by Wright's eschatology remains, in my opinion, the most significant outcome of his thought. Humility is needed from both evangelicals and liberals here, as acceptance of this theology requires both 'sides' to recognize that a high Christology and the radical social mission of the Church are inextricably entwined. Speaking as an evangelical, however, I do believe that the challenge in the first instance lies with evangelicals to demonstrate that credal orthodoxy is truly radical rather than oriented to the status quo. If this can happen then it is possible that the disastrous schism towards which the Anglican Communion is currently moving can yet be averted. The Christian response to homosexuality will, of course, remain an utterly divisive issue. However, if evangelicals can be at the forefront of fighting injustice, there is far less chance of liberals seeing a conservative stance on homosexual practice as simply another instrument of oppression. The development of a really positive theology of creation will help here since it will demonstrate that evangelical concerns about homosexuality are based on a well thought out and sincere theology for the leading of fully human lives rather than the reactionary employment of a few arbitrary 'proof texts'. From this basis, a properly pastoral response that aims to 'meet people where they are', based upon humility and careful listening, may win respect from those who still cannot agree with its premise. Obviously this will not be nearly enough to lead to an easy resolution of this utterly complex issue. But it will provide a far more secure basis for what many are now starting to realize is a conversation waiting to begin.[14]

The theology of Tom Wright has, therefore, emerged at a really vital moment for the Church. Christians everywhere face the challenge that Wright has issued to review the inadequate aspects of our traditions in the light of his fresh and explosive interpretation of Jesus, Paul and the rest of the New Testament. It would be much easier and seemingly safer to continue the avoidance of engaging with Wright's theology that many at both ends of the theological spectrum appear to be determined to maintain. But for the sake of the worship, mission and unity of the Church in the twenty-first century, it is vital that this proper engagement occurs.

Notes

Preface

1 See <www.ccnm.org>.

2 Stephen Kuhrt, *Church Growth Through the Full Welcome of Children: The Sssh Free Church*, Grove Evangelism Series No. 87 (Cambridge: Grove Books, 2009).

3 Wright's own attempt to encourage this can be particularly found in his *New Tasks for a Renewed Church* (London: Hodder/Bloomington, MN: Bethany House, 1992).

1 The career of Tom Wright: emergence, scholarship and non-engagement

1 John Cheeseman, Philip Gardner, Michael Sadgrove and Tom Wright, *The Grace of God in the Gospel* (Edinburgh: Banner of Truth, 1972).

2 E. P. Sanders, *Paul and Palestinian Judaism: A Comparison of Patterns of Religion* (London: SCM Press/Philadelphia: Fortress, 1977). See also Sanders' *Paul, the Law and the Jewish People* (Philadelphia: Fortress/ London: SCM Press, 1983) and *Paul*, Past Masters (Oxford: Oxford University Press, 1991). For a brief and but helpful introduction to the 'new perspective' and summaries of the contributions to this of Sanders, J. D. G. Dunn and Wright see Michael B. Thompson, *The New Perspective on Paul*, Grove Biblical Series No. 26 (Cambridge: Grove Books, 2002).

3 A further area of Wright's earliest research was the works of the Protestant Reformer John Frith (d. 1533). Wright published the first complete edition in *The Work of John Frith*, Courtenay Library of Reformation Classics No. 7 (Appleford: Sutton Courtenay Press, 1983).

4 With Michael Sadgrove, Chapter 3, 'Jesus Christ the Only Saviour', in J. R. W. Stott (ed.), *Obeying Christ in a Changing World*, Vol 1: *The Lord Christ* (London: Collins, 1977).

5 *Evangelical Anglican Identity: The Connection Between Bible, Gospel and Church*, Latimer Studies No. 8 (Oxford: Latimer, 1980). This was later republished, with two previous Latimer studies by J. I. Packer, in *Anglican Evangelical Identity: Yesterday and Today* (London: Latimer Trust, 2008).

6 Wright's first major academic article was 'The Paul of History and the Apostle of Faith', published in *Tyndale Bulletin*, 29, 1978, which can also be found at: <www.ntwrightpage.com/Wright_Paul_History.pdf>.

7 *Small Faith, Great God* (Eastbourne: Kingsway/New Jersey: Revell, 1978).

8 *The Epistles of Paul to the Colossians and to Philemon* (Leicester: Tyndale/ Grand Rapids, MI: Eerdmans, 1986).

9 *The Interpretation of the New Testament 1861–1986*, with Stephen Neill (Oxford: Oxford University Press, 1988). Neill died in 1984 while the work on this revision was still being completed.

10 The series commenced with the first volume, *The New Testament and the People of God* (London: SPCK/Minneapolis: Fortress, 1992); followed by *Jesus and the Victory of God* (London: SPCK/Minneapolis: Fortress, 1996).

11 *The Original Jesus* (Oxford: Lion/Grand Rapids, MI: Eerdmans, 1996); *The Challenge of Jesus* (Downers Grove, IL: Inter-Varsity Press/London: SPCK, 1999).

12 *Who Was Jesus?* (London: SPCK/Grand Rapids, MI: Eerdmans, 1992). As part of his engagement with other Jesus scholars, Wright also published, in dialogue with Marcus J. Borg, *The Meaning of Jesus: Two Visions* (San Francisco: Harper San Francisco/London: SPCK, 1999). See also *Jesus and the Victory of God*, ch. 2.

13 The exhortation to 'take Tom with a pinch of salt' was made to me by the New Testament scholar Professor David Catchpole in a conversation prior to the start of my ordination training in 2000.

14 *New Heavens, New Earth: The Biblical Picture of the Christian Hope*, Grove Biblical Series No. 11 (Cambridge: Grove Books, 1999); *The Resurrection of the Son of God*, Vol. 3 of *Christian Origins and the Question of God* (London: SPCK/Minneapolis: Fortress, 2003).

15 *Surprised by Hope* (London: SPCK, 2007); US edition has the subtitle *Rethinking Heaven, Resurrection and the Mission of the Church* (San Francisco: Harper One, 2008).

16 Wright's views on eschatology were also published in *The Myth of the Millennium* (London: SPCK/Louisville, KY: Westminster, 1999). On the resurrection, see also *The Resurrection of Jesus: John Dominic Crossan and N. T. Wright in Dialogue*, ed. Robert B. Stewart (Minneapolis: Fortress, 2006).

17 *Paul and the Faithfulness of God*, Vol. 4 of *Christian Origins and the Question of God* (London: SPCK/Minneapolis: Fortress, forthcoming 2011).

18 *The Climax of the Covenant: Christ and the Law in Pauline Theology* (Edinburgh: T & T Clark, 1991/Minneapolis: Fortress, 1992).

19 *What St Paul Really Said* (Oxford: Lion/Grand Rapids, MI: Eerdmans, 1997).

20 *Romans*, in *The New Interpreter's Bible*, Vol. X, 393–770 (Nashville, TN: Abingdon, 2002); *Paul: Fresh Perspectives* (London: SPCK/Minneapolis: Fortress, 2005).

21 John Piper, *The Future of Justification: A Response to N. T. Wright* (Nottingham, Inter-Varsity Press, 2008).

22 *Justification: God's Plan and Paul's Vision* (London: SPCK/Downers Grove, IL: Inter-Varsity Press, 2009).

23 *New Tasks for a Renewed Church* (London: Hodder/Bloomington, MN: Bethany House, 1992); *The Lord and his Prayer* (London: SPCK/Grand Rapids, MI: Eerdmans, 1996); *For All God's Worth* (London: SPCK/Grand Rapids, MI: Eerdmans, 1997); *Holy Communion for Amateurs* (London: Hodder/Louisville, KY: Westminster John Knox, 1999, reissued as *The Meal Jesus Gave Us*, 2002). Other more popular level books include *The Crown and the Fire* (London: SPCK/Grand Rapids, MI: Eerdmans, 1992); *Following Jesus: Biblical Reflections on Christian Discipleship* (London: SPCK/Grand Rapids, MI: Eerdmans, 1994); *The Way of the Lord: Christian Pilgrimage in the Holy Land and Beyond* (London: SPCK/Grand Rapids, MI: Eerdmans, 1999); *The Cross and the Colliery* (London: SPCK/Ijamsville, MD: The Word Among Us Press, 2007).

24 The *For Everyone* series began with *Mark for Everyone* and *Luke for Everyone* (both London: SPCK/Louisville, KY: Westminster John Knox, 2001).

25 This series began with *Lent for Everyone: Luke* (London: SPCK, 2009). Wright also published reflections on the passages set in the Church of England's Common Worship Revised Lectionary in *Twelve Months of Sundays: Reflections on Bible Readings* (London: SPCK, 2000 (Year C), 2001 (Year A), and 2002 (Year B)).

26 *Simply Christian* (London: SPCK/San Francisco: Harper San Francisco, 2006); *Scripture and the Authority of God* (London: SPCK/San Francisco: Harper San Francisco, 2005); *Evil and the Justice of God* (London: SPCK/Downers Grove, IL: Inter-Varsity Press, 2006); *Judas and the Gospel of Jesus* (London: SPCK/Grand Rapids, MI: Baker Books, 2006); *Virtue Reborn* (London: SPCK/San Francisco: Harper One, 2010).

27 Most of Wright's articles can be found at <www.ntwrightpage.com>.

28 The Windsor Report can be found at <www.anglicancommunion.org/windsor2004/index.cfm>.

29 See <www.fulcrum-anglican.org.uk>. Wright's articles published on the Fulcrum website can be found at: <www.fulcrum-anglican.org.uk/pageinfo.cfm?author=Tom Wright>.

30 A full bibliography including Wright's interviews, broadcasts and newspaper articles can be found at: <www.ntwrightpage.com/NTW_Publications.htm>. A number of these together with recordings of lectures by Wright can also be accessed on the same website.

31 A good (or bad) example of this is found in *Christology and the New Testament: Jesus and his Earliest Followers* by the Oxford scholar Christopher M. Tuckett (Edinburgh: Edinburgh University Press, 2001). Although published in 2001, Tuckett's book shows no evidence whatsoever that he was aware of Wright's work; Wright's books are noticeably absent from the bibliography and his name is not included in the list of 125 other modern scholars cited (see pp. 234–40).

32 *New Heavens, New Earth*, p. 25.

33 Piper, *The Future of Justification*.

34 *Justification*, particularly pp. 3–36, 45–52.

35 Steve Jeffrey, Mike Ovey and Andrew Sach, *Pierced for Our Transgressions: Rediscovering the Glory of Penal Substitution* (Nottingham: Inter-Varsity Press, 2007).

36 'The Cross and the Caricatures: A Response to Robert Jenson, Jeffrey John and a new volume called *Pierced for Our Transgressions*', at: <www.fulcrum-anglican.org.uk/news/2007/20070423wright.cfm?doc=205>.

37 Jeffrey, Ovey and Sach, *Pierced for Our Transgressions*, pp. 85–6, 93–4, 312.

38 See note 4 above.

39 J. R. W. Stott, *'What is the Spirit saying . . .': A Report on NEAC3* (London: Church of England Evangelical Council, 1988), p. 3.

40 See the pre-NEAC4 book *Fanning the Flame: Bible, Cross and Mission: Meeting the Challenge in a Changing World*, ed. Paul Gardner, Chris Wright and Chris Green (Grand Rapids, MI: Zondervan, 2003).

41 T. Dudley-Smith, *John Stott: A Global Ministry* (Leicester: Inter-Varsity Press, 2001), ch. 7.

42 See <www.lausanne.org>.

2 Theological questions awaiting an answer . . .

1 For an account of this see Christopher Sandford, *McQueen: The Biography* (London: Harper Collins, 2001), pp. 399–457.

2 J. R. W. Stott, *The Authentic Jesus: A Response to Current Scepticism in the Church* (Basingstoke: Marshall Pickering, 1985).

3 Stott, *The Authentic Jesus*, p. 52.

4 Section 6 of the Lausanne Covenant declared, 'In the Church's mission of sacrificial service, evangelism is primary.' Billy Graham's endorsement of Christians working for social justice including the reform of unfair social structures was also accompanied by his comment that working for social justice is 'not our priority mission'. See 'Why Lausanne?' in J. D. Douglas (ed.) *Let the Earth Hear His Voice: International Congress on World Evangelisation, Lausanne, Switzerland* (Minneapolis: World Wide Publications, 1975), p. 29.

5 See J. R. W. Stott, *New Issues Facing Christians Today* (London: Collins/ Marshall Pickering, 1999), ch. 1 particularly pp. 17–32. See also Ronald J. Sider, with a Response by John R. W. Stott, *Evangelism, Salvation and Social Justice*, Grove Ethics Series No. 16 (Bramcote: Grove Books, 1977), pp. 21–4.

6 *Evangelism and Social Responsibility: An Evangelical Commitment* (Grand Rapids, MI: Eerdmans, 1982), p. 23. See also J. R. W. Stott, '*What is the Spirit saying . . .*': *A Report on NEAC3* (London: Church of England Evangelical Council, 1988), p. 6.

7 The same logic can be seen in John Stott's comments on 'the greater importance of the eternal' with the assumption that this would include the results of evangelism but not social action. See Sider, *Evangelism, Salvation and Social Justice*, pp. 21–2.

8 Many of the thoughts in this section have been developed through conversations with my brother Jon Kuhrt. See his article, 'What Evangelicals have done to Sin', at: <www.fulcrum-anglican.org.uk/ news/2006/20060321kuhrt.cfm?doc=94>.

9 Dudley-Smith, *John Stott*, p. 27.

10 See <www.christiansinsport.org.uk>.

11 H. Richard Niebuhr, *Christ and Culture* (New York: Harper Collins, 1951). Examples of recent more popular books encouraging theological reflection upon novels and films include Connie Neal, *The Gospel According to Harry Potter* (Louisville, KY: John Knox Press, 2002) and M. Stibbe and J. John, *Passion for the Movies* (Milton Keynes: Authentic, 2005).

12 See <www.greenbelt.org.uk>.

13 P. Crowe, *Keele '67 – the National Evangelical Anglican Congress Statement* (London: Falcon Books, 1967), p. 35.

14 Much of this influence of Colin Buchanan was conveyed through his prolific output of Grove books in the Worship series (see <www.

grovebooks.co.uk>). See also Buchanan's chapter, 'Doctrine and Worship' in Gordon Kuhrt (ed.) *Doctrine Matters* (London: Hodder, 1993).

15 Crowe, *Keele '67*, p. 35.

16 See, for example, Stephen Cottrell, *Sacrament, Wholeness and Evangelism: A Catholic Approach*, Grove Evangelism Series No. 33 (Cambridge: Grove Books, 1996).

17 Quoted in Stott, *'What is the Spirit saying . . .'*, p. 8.

18 See, for instance, Melvin Tinker, 'Towards an evangelical view of the Church', in *The Anglican Evangelical Crisis: A Radical Agenda for a Bible Based Church*, ed. Melvin Tinker (Fearn: Christian Focus, 1995).

19 See particularly Dave Tomlinson, *The Post Evangelical* (London: Triangle, 1995), and Graham Cray et al., *The Post Evangelical Debate* (London: Triangle, 1997).

20 Steve Chalke and Alan Mann, *The Lost Message of Jesus* (Grand Rapids, MI: Zondervan, 2003).

3 A summary of the theology of N. T. Wright

1 The description of Wright's style used on the Ship of Fools website and quoted on the cover of the *For Everyone* series of commentaries.

2 My defence for the rampant mix of metaphors in these two paragraphs ('bridges', 'pennies', 'building blocks' and 'pegs'!) is Wright's enjoyment of St Paul's tendency to do much the same in his similar eagerness to communicate! See *Paul for Everyone: Galatians and Thessalonians* (London: SPCK/Louisville, KY: Westminster John Knox, 2002), p. 127; *Paul for Everyone: The Prison Letters* (London: SPCK/Louisville, KY: Westminster John Knox, 2002), p. 47.

3 *The New Testament and the People of God* (London: SPCK/Minneapolis: Fortress, 1992) (*NTPG*), pp. 60, 92–5; *Jesus and the Victory of God* (London: SPCK/Minneapolis: Fortress, 1996) (*JVG*), pp. 8–10, 117; *The Challenge of Jesus* (Downers Grove, IL: Inter-Varsity Press/London: SPCK, 1999), ch. 1; *The Resurrection of the Son of God* (London: SPCK/Minneapolis: Fortress, 2003) (*RSG*), pp. 28–31; *The Meaning of Jesus: Two Visions* with Marcus J. Borg (San Francisco: Harper San Francisco/London: SPCK, 1999), pp. 15–17.

4 *NTPG*, pp. 10, 88.

5 *NTPG*, p. 97; *JVG*, p. xiv; *Challenge of Jesus*, pp. 3–13; *Meaning of Jesus*, pp. 17, 26–7.

6 *NTPG*, pp. 10, 97, 149; *Simply Christian* (London: SPCK/San Francisco: Harper San Francisco, 2006), p. 81; *New Tasks for a Renewed Church* (London: Hodder/Bloomington, MN: Bethany House, 1992), p. 175.

7 *JVG*, p. 23; *Challenge of Jesus*, p. 7.

8 *Challenge of Jesus*, p. 134; *Following Jesus: Biblical Reflections on Christian Discipleship* (London: SPCK/Grand Rapids, MI: Eerdmans, 1994), p. ix. For Wright's similar emphasis upon the importance of understanding Paul in his historical context see particularly *Justification: God's Plan and Paul's Vision* (London: SPCK/Downers Grove, IL: Inter-Varsity Press, 2009), pp. 20–1, 30–6, 59–65.

9 *JVG*, pp. 28–82; *Meaning of Jesus*, pp. 23–4.

10 *JVG*, p. 88.

11 *NTPG*, pp. 81–120; *JVG*, p. 133; *Challenge of Jesus*, p. 15; *Meaning of Jesus*, pp. 22–3.

12 *NTPG*, pp. 339–464.

13 *NTPG*, p. 448; *JVG*, pp. 109–12, 120.

14 *NTPG*, pp. 32, 38–45.

15 *NTPG*, pp. 109–12, 122–6; *JVG*, pp. 137–44.

16 *NTPG*, pp. 109–12; *JVG*, pp. 137–44; *Challenge of Jesus*, p. 53.

17 *Simply Christian*, ch. 6; *Evil and the Justice of God* (London: SPCK/Downers Grove, IL: Inter-Varsity Press, 2006) (*EJG*), pp. 22–44. For Wright's similar emphasis upon the importance of the story of Israel in Paul's theology see *Justification*, pp. 17–21; *The Climax of the Covenant: Christ and the Law in Pauline Theology* (Edinburgh: T & T Clark, 1991/Minneapolis: Fortress, 1992), particularly ch. 14.

18 See particularly 'The Cross and the Caricatures: A Response to Robert Jenson, Jeffrey John and a new volume called *Pierced for Our Transgressions*', at: <www.fulcrum-anglican.org.uk/news/2007/20070423wright. cfm?doc=205>.

19 *NTPG*, pp. 150, 157–61, 216–23; *Challenge of Jesus*, pp. 29–30. For a similar emphasis upon the importance of 'the story of Israel' in Paul's theology see *Justification*, pp. 17–21.

20 *NTPG*, pp. 259–68; *Simply Christian*, pp. 64–5; *What St Paul Really Said* (Oxford: Lion/Grand Rapids, MI: Eerdmans, 1997), p. 118; *Paul: Fresh Perspectives* (London: SPCK/Minneapolis: Fortress, 2005), pp. 21–6, 108–10; *New Tasks*, pp. 40–1.

21 *New Tasks*, p. 41.

22 *NTPG*, p. 259; *What St Paul Really Said*, pp. 63–5; *Challenge of Jesus*, pp. 74–5; *Meaning of Jesus*, p. 31; *New Tasks*, p. 17.

23 *NTPG*, pp. 248–59; *Challenge of Jesus*, p. 74; *Meaning of Jesus*, pp. 159–60; *Paul: Fresh Perspectives*, pp. 86–90.

24 *What St Paul Really Said*, ch. 6; *Paul: Fresh Perspectives*, pp. 25–6.

25 *NTPG*, pp. 227–41, 262; *Simply Christian*, pp. 71–2; *New Tasks*, p. 42; *Justification*, pp. 53–8.

26 *NTPG*, pp. 224–6; *JVG*, pp. 405–12; *New Tasks*, pp. 19–20.

27 *Simply Christian*, p. 65.

28 *New Tasks*, pp. 46–7; *EJG*, pp. 29–35.

29 *Simply Christian*, pp. 66–8; *New Tasks*, p. 44.

30 *Paul: Fresh Perspectives*, p. 22; *New Tasks*, p. 43.

31 *NTPG*, pp. 291–7; *Simply Christian*, pp. 75–6; *EJG*, pp. 36–9; *New Tasks*, pp. 44–5.

32 *NTPG*, pp. 268–79; *JVG*, pp. xvii–xviii, 126–9, 204–6; *Challenge of Jesus*, pp. 19–20; *Meaning of Jesus*, p. 32; *Simply Christian*, pp. 68–9; *Paul: Fresh Perspectives*, p. 133; *Justification*, pp. 41–5; *New Tasks*, p. 47.

33 *JVG*, pp. 615–31; *Challenge of Jesus*, pp. 76–8; *What St Paul Really Said*, pp. 41–4.

34 *Simply Christian*, p. 71.

35 *NTPG*, ch. 10; *Paul: Fresh Perspectives*, p. 132; *Scripture and the Authority of God* (London: SPCK/San Francisco: Harper San Francisco, 2005), p. 30.

36 *NTPG*, pp. 169–70, 294, 299–307; *Paul: Fresh Perspectives*, pp. 131–5; *Justification*, pp. 35–40.

37 *NTPG*, pp. 280–6; *Challenge of Jesus*, p. 21; *Paul: Fresh Perspectives*, pp. 41–2.

38 *NTPG*, pp. 280–338, particularly 332–4.

39 *NTPG*, pp. 280–6, 425.

40 *What St Paul Really Said*, pp. 40–4.

41 *NTPG*, pp. 319–20; *JVG*, pp. 481–6; *Challenge of Jesus*, p. 53; *Simply Christian*, pp. 70, 73, 90–1; *Paul: Fresh Perspectives*, pp. 42–3.

42 *NTPG*, pp. 170–214; *Challenge of Jesus*, p. 20.

43 *NTPG*, pp. 267–8.

44 *NTPG*, pp. 297–9; *Meaning of Jesus*, pp. 200–1; *Following Jesus*, ch. 11; *Simply Christian*, pp. 56–9.

45 *Paul: Fresh Perspectives*, pp. 50–1; *New Heavens, New Earth: The Biblical Picture of Christian Hope*, Grove Biblical Series No. 11 (Cambridge: Grove Books, 1999), p. 15; see also 'heaven' in the glossary included at the end of each of the *For Everyone* commentaries, e.g. *Mark for Everyone* (London: SPCK/Louisville, KY: Westminster John Knox, 2001), p. 232.

46 *Simply Christian*, pp. 72–5.

47 *NTPG*, pp. 200, 211, 320–34; *Challenge of Jesus*, pp. 100–3; *Meaning of Jesus*, pp. 113–14; *RSG*, pp. 200–2.

48 *RSG*, pp. 150–3, 202–6; *Meaning of Jesus*, p. 113.

49 *Surprised by Hope* (London: SPCK, 2007/San Francisco: Harper One, 2008), pp. 86–7.

50 *NTPG*, pp. 211–12; *Meaning of Jesus*, p. 112; *RSG*, pp. 131–40, 485, 503; *Surprised by Hope*, pp. 225–6.

51 *NTPG*, pp. 215–38; *JVG*, pp. 383–405; *New Tasks*, pp. 19–20.

52 *NTPG*, pp. 237–41; *Justification*, pp. 53–7, 96; *New Tasks*, p. 18.

53 *JVG*, pp. 145–97; *Challenge of Jesus*, p. 22; *Meaning of Jesus*, p. 33; *Simply Christian*, p. 91; *New Tasks*, p. 49.

54 *JVG*, pp. 166–7.

55 *JVG*, pp. 163–7.

56 *JVG*, pp. 172, 191–6; 268–74; *Challenge of Jesus*, pp. 22–5; *Simply Christian*, pp. 85–7.

57 *JVG*, pp. 191–4.

58 *Challenge of Jesus*, p. 47; *Simply Christian*, p. 88; *New Tasks*, pp. 67–8.

59 *Challenge of Jesus*, p. 38.

60 *JVG*, pp. 305–10.

61 *JVG*, ch. 9; *Challenge of Jesus*, ch. 3; *Meaning of Jesus*, pp. 42–4; *Simply Christian*, p. 88.

62 *Challenge of Jesus*, pp. 26–7, 46–7; *Meaning of Jesus*, pp. 38–9; *Scripture and the Authority of God*, p. 80. See also 'Communion and Koinonia: Pauline Reflections on Tolerance and Boundaries', paper given by N. T. Wright to the Future of Anglicanism Conference, Oxford, 2002, at: <www.ntwrightpage.com/Wright_Communion_Koinonia.htm>.

63 *JVG*, pp. 246–58; *Challenge of Jesus*, pp. 25–9; *Meaning of Jesus*, pp. 35, 38.

64 *JVG*, pp. 287–97; *Challenge of Jesus*, pp. 27–9; *EJG*, p. 52; *Virtue Reborn* (London: SPCK/San Francisco: Harper One, 2010), pp. 88–9.

65 *JVG*, pp. 304; *Challenge of Jesus*, pp. 26–8, 30; *Meaning of Jesus*, p. 39.

66 *JVG*, p. 432; *Challenge of Jesus*, p. 48.

67 *JVG*, pp. 283–7; *Meaning of Jesus*, p. 39; *Virtue Reborn*, pp. 103–9.

68 *JVG*, pp. 130–1; *Challenge of Jesus*, p. 28; *Meaning of Jesus*, p. 45.

69 *JVG*, pp. 257–8; *Challenge of Jesus*, pp. 27, 82; *Meaning of Jesus*, pp. 46–7.

70 *JVG*, pp. 195–6, 201, 446–3; *Meaning of Jesus*, pp. 36, 48; *New Tasks*, pp. 68; *EJG*, p. 49.

71 *JVG*, pp. 296–91, 447; *Challenge of Jesus*, p. 28; *New Tasks*, p. 48; *Following Jesus*, ch. 5.

72 *JVG*, pp. 457–9; *New Tasks*, pp. 22–5.

73 *JVG*, p. 304; *Challenge of Jesus*, p. 30; *New Tasks*, p. 66; *EJG*, p. 52.

74 *JVG*, p. 178.

75 *JVG*, pp. 174–82.

76 *JVG*, pp. 230–9; *Challenge of Jesus*, pp. 22–4. See also the work of Ken Bailey, particularly *Jacob and the Prodigal: How Jesus Retold Israel's Story* (Oxford: Bible Reading Fellowship/Downers Grove, IL: Inter-Varsity Press, 2003).

77 *JVG*, pp. 631–45; *Challenge of Jesus*, pp. 86–8; *Surprised by Hope*, p. 138.

78 *JVG*, pp. 202–9, ch. 8; *Challenge of Jesus*, pp. 30–2; *Meaning of Jesus*, pp. 40–1.

79 *JVG*, pp. 413–28; *Challenge of Jesus*, pp. 42–6; *Meaning of Jesus*, p. 45; *New Tasks*, p. 69.

80 *NTPG*, ch. 10; *Meaning of Jesus*, pp. 41–2; *The Myth of the Millennium* (London: SPCK/Louisville, KY: Westminster, 1999), ch. 2.

81 *New Heavens, New Earth*, p. 8.

82 *JVG*, pp. 339–67; *Challenge of Jesus*, pp. 31–2.

83 *JVG*, pp. 360–5; *Challenge of Jesus*, p. 32, *Surprised by Hope*, pp. 137–8.

84 *JVG*, pp. 490–528; *Challenge of Jesus*, pp. 54–8; *Meaning of Jesus*, pp. 47–51.

85 *JVG*, pp. 530–7.

86 *JVG*, ch. 12.

87 *JVG*, p. 588.

88 *JVG*, pp. 576–92; *Meaning of Jesus*, p. 94; *New Tasks*, p. 20.

89 *JVG*, pp. 554–63, 604–9; *Challenge of Jesus*, pp. 59–61.

90 *The Crown and the Fire* (London: SPCK/Grand Rapids, MI: Eerdmans, 1992), pp. x–xi; *EJG*, pp. 47–8.

91 *JVG*, pp. 592–611; *Crown and the Fire*, pp. 18–20; *New Tasks*, p. 71; *EJG*, pp. 51–2.

92 *Crown and the Fire*, Part One; *New Tasks*, pp. 71–3; *EJG*, pp. 48–50, 52–5, 57–8.

93 *New Tasks*, pp. 80–1; *EJG*, pp. 55–8.

94 'The Cross and the Caricatures'.

95 *EJG*, p. 59.

96 *JVG*, pp. 612–53; *Challenge of Jesus*, ch. 5; *Meaning of Jesus*, ch. 10; *Simply Christian*, pp. 101–2.

97 *Challenge of Jesus*, p. 86; *EJG*, pp. 52–3.

98 *JVG*, pp. 362, 394, 413–28; *Challenge of Jesus*, pp. 42, 60, 81–6; *New Tasks*, pp. 68–9.

99 *JVG*, pp. 524–8, 642–4; *Challenge of Jesus*, pp. 88–9.

100 *JVG*, pp. 652–3; *Challenge of Jesus*, pp. 90–3; *Meaning of Jesus*, p. 166; *Simply Christian*, p. 102.

101 *RSG*, pp. 571–8.
102 *Simply Christian*, pp. 100–1.
103 *Meaning of Jesus*, pp. 117–19; *RSG*, pp. 559–63; *Surprised by Hope*, pp. 64–9; *Simply Christian*, pp. 99–100.
104 *Meaning of Jesus*, pp. 122–3; *RSG*, pp. 587–682; *Surprised by Hope*, pp. 64–9; *Simply Christian*, p. 97.
105 *NTPG*, pp. 181–203, particularly 200; *What St Paul Really Said*, pp. 25–35; *Meaning of Jesus*, pp. 112–13.
106 *What St Paul Really Said*, pp. 36, 50; *Challenge of Jesus*, pp. 106–10; *Meaning of Jesus*, pp. 119–20, 126; *RSG*, pp. 375–98; *Paul: Fresh Perspectives*, pp. 26–39, 136–7; *Justification*, pp. 79–81, 84–5.
107 *What St Paul Really Said*, pp. 36–7, 51–5; *Meaning of Jesus*, p. 125; *Justification*, p. 189.
108 *What St Paul Really Said*, pp. 37, 82; *Paul: Fresh Perspectives*, p. 69.
109 *What St Paul Really Said*, pp. 41–4; *Challenge of Jesus*, p. 25.
110 Stated particularly emphatically in the introduction to each of the *For Everyone* series of commentaries; see *Mark for Everyone*, pp. ix–x.
111 *New Tasks*, pp. 161–9; *Following Jesus*, p. 95; *Surprised by Hope*, chs 12–13.
112 *What St Paul Really Said*, ch. 1; and the whole thrust of *Paul: Fresh Perspectives*.
113 *What St Paul Really Said*, pp. 79–83; *Paul: Fresh Perspectives*, pp. 163–4.
114 *What St Paul Really Said*, pp. 87, 136–40.
115 *What St Paul Really Said*, p. 89, ch. 8.
116 *What St Paul Really Said*, pp. 116–17; *Paul: Fresh Perspectives*, p. 121.
117 *What St Paul Really Said*, p. 117; *Paul: Fresh Perspectives*, pp. 121–2.
118 *What St Paul Really Said*, pp. 47–9; *EJG*, p. 59.
119 *Climax of the Covenant*; *EJG*, p. 59; *Paul: Fresh Perspectives*, pp. 40–50.
120 *Climax of the Covenant*, ch. 10; *Paul: Fresh Perspectives*, p. 36.
121 *Climax of the Covenant*, ch. 11; *What St Paul Really Said*, p. 50; *EJG*, p. 55.
122 *EJG*, p. 55.
123 The whole thrust of *EJG*.
124 'The Cross and the Caricatures'; *EJG*, p. 60. 'The wrath of God is satisfied' is a line contained in the 2001 hymn 'In Christ alone' by Stuart Townend and Keith Getty.
125 *NTPG*, pp. 271–2; *What St Paul Really Said*, ch. 6; *Justification*, pp. 72–9.

126 *What St Paul Really Said*, pp. 96–9; *Justification*, pp. 49–51, 65–72.

127 *What St Paul Really Said*, pp. 84, 127; *Paul: Fresh Perspectives*, pp. 29, 47; *Justification*, pp. 169–75.

128 *What St Paul Really Said*, p. 84; *Paul: Fresh Perspectives*, pp. 30–1, 47, 53, 110–20; *Justification*, pp. 176–90.

129 *Paul: Fresh Perspectives*, pp. 30–1; *Paul for Everyone: Romans* (London: SPCK/Louisville, KY: Westminster John Knox, 2004); 'Romans and the Theology of Paul', in *Pauline Theology, Vol. III*, ed. David M. Hay and E. Elizabeth Johnson (Minneapolis: Fortress, 1995), also at: <www.ntwrightpage.com/Wright_Romans_Theology_Paul.pdf>.

130 *NTPG*, p. 238; *What St Paul Really Said*, pp. 118–20; *Justification*, pp. 53–8.

131 *What St Paul Really Said*, pp. 120–9; *Paul: Fresh Perspectives*, pp. 113–14, 121–2, 125–9.

132 *Justification*, p. 110.

133 *New Tasks*, pp. 167–8; *Justification*, pp. 91–118.

134 *What St Paul Really Said*, p. 138; *Justification*, pp. 115, 120.

135 *What St Paul Really Said*, pp. 157–9; *Paul: Fresh Perspectives*, pp. 112–13, 159–60; *New Tasks*, pp. 167–8. In overall terms, Wright is nonetheless very clear that rather than 'advancing ecclesiology over soteriology', he is simply emphasizing the crucial role of the Church in God's plan of salvation. See *Justification*, pp. 124, 219 and the whole thrust of *Evangelical Anglican Identity: The Connection between Bible, Gospel and Church*, Latimer Studies No. 8 (Oxford: Latimer, 1980; republished in *Anglican Evangelical Identity: Yesterday and Today*, 2008), particularly pp. 89–120.

136 *What St Paul Really Said*, pp. 119, 122–3; *Paul: Fresh Perspectives*, pp. 46–7, 113; *Justification*, pp. 29–30, 47, 84, 114, 119, 127–8, 133–44, 180–1, 187, 205–9.

137 *What St Paul Really Said*, p. 70; *Challenge of Jesus*, p. 52, 79; *Simply Christian*, p. 100; *Paul: Fresh Perspectives*, p. 48.

138 *What St Paul Really Said*, p. 71; *Meaning of Jesus*, p. 163; *RSG*, pp. 571–8; *Paul: Fresh Perspectives*, p. 48; *Crown and the Fire*, ch. 7.

139 *Climax of the Covenant*, chs 2–6; *NTPG*, pp. 448–9; *What St Paul Really Said*, pp. 65–72; *Meaning of Jesus*, pp. 161–3; *RSG*, pp. 397–8; *Paul: Fresh Perspectives*, pp. 91–6.

140 *What St Paul Really Said*, pp. 72–4; *Paul: Fresh Perspectives*, pp. 97–101.

141 *What St Paul Really Said*, p. 72; *Meaning of Jesus*, pp. 160–3; *Challenge of Jesus*, pp. 75, 77–8; *Simply Christian*, pp. 76–7; *New Tasks*, p. 98; *Justification*, pp. 132–3.

142 *Paul: Fresh Perspectives*, p. 102; *Justification*, p. 115.

143 *Paul: Fresh Perspectives*, p. 99.

144 *What St Paul Really Said*, pp. 56–7, 88; *Meaning of Jesus*, pp. 219–21; RSG, pp. 568–70; *Paul: Fresh Perspectives*, ch. 4.

145 *Paul: Fresh Perspectives*, pp. 5, 62–9.

146 *What St Paul Really Said*, p. 57; *Paul: Fresh Perspectives*, pp. 71–9; *New Tasks*, p. 80.

147 *Paul: Fresh Perspectives*, pp. 78–9.

148 *Luke for Everyone* (London: SPCK/Louisville, KY: Westminster John Knox, 2001), pp. 22–4.

149 'Shipwreck and Kingdom: Acts and the Anglican Communion', closing address at the 13th meeting of the Anglican Consultative Council, in *Living Communion: The Official Report of the 13th Meeting of the Anglican Consultative Council, Nottingham 2005*, ed. J. M. Rosenthal and S. T. Erdey (New York: Church Publishing Incorporated, 2006), pp. 106–18. Also at: <www.fulcrum-anglican.org.uk/news/2005/20050628wright.cfm?doc= 116>; *Following Jesus*, ch. 11.

150 'Shipwreck and Kingdom'.

151 'Shipwreck and Kingdom'.

152 *Following Jesus*, ch. 12; 'Shipwreck and Kingdom'.

153 *Paul: Fresh Perspectives*, pp. 78–9.

154 *Meaning of Jesus*, p. 22; *Simply Christian*, p. 83; *Judas and the Gospel of Jesus* (London: SPCK/Grand Rapids, MI: Baker Books, 2006); *Scripture and the Authority of God*), pp. 47–8.

155 *Paul: Fresh Perspectives*, p. 73.

156 *Paul: Fresh Perspectives*, p. 142; *Surprised by Hope*, p. 141.

157 *Paul: Fresh Perspectives*, pp. 54–5, 143; *Surprised by Hope*, pp. 147–9.

158 *Meaning of Jesus*, pp. 202–4; *Paul: Fresh Perspectives*, p. 144; *Surprised by Hope*, pp. 112–19, 160–1, 171–6.

159 *Paul: Fresh Perspectives*, p. 143; and the major thrust of *Surprised by Hope* and *New Heavens, New Earth*.

160 RSG, pp. 464–7; *Surprised by Hope*, pp. 163–4; *New Heavens, New Earth*, pp. 7–8.

161 *Surprised by Hope*, pp. 111–12; *New Heavens, New Earth*, p. 8.

162 *Surprised by Hope*, pp. 162–3.

163 *Surprised by Hope*, pp. 150–1.

164 *Paul: Fresh Perspectives*, pp. 143–4; *Surprised by Hope*, p. 152; *Justification*, pp. 86, 158–68.

165 John Piper, *The Future of Justification: A Response to N. T. Wright* (Nottingham: Inter-Varsity Press, 2008), ch. 7.

166 *Paul: Fresh Perspectives*, p. 148; *Justification*, pp. 181–5.

167 *Surprised by Hope*, p. 157.

168 *Following Jesus*, ch. 10; *Surprised by Hope*, pp. 187–96; *For All the Saints? Remembering the Christian Departed* (London: SPCK/Harrisburg, PA: Morehouse, 2003), pp. 42–6.

169 *EJG*, chs 4–5; *Surprised by Hope*, Part 3; and the whole thrust of *Virtue Reborn*.

170 *Paul: Fresh Perspectives*, p. 146; *Simply Christian*, pp. 104–5.

171 *Challenge of Jesus*, pp. 138–41; *EJG*, pp. 64–5.

172 *Paul: Fresh Perspectives*, p. 147.

173 *Challenge of Jesus*, pp. 141–2; *EJG*, pp. 90–1; *Surprised by Hope*, pp. 172–4; *Virtue Reborn*, ch. 3.

174 *Virtue Reborn*, pp. 83–7.

175 *Paul: Fresh Perspectives*, p. 122; *Justification*, pp. 26–7, 149–50.

176 The whole thrust of *Evangelical Anglican Identity: The Connection between Bible, Gospel and Church*. Wright's influence was also crucial in ensuring that 'Church' joined 'Gospel' and 'Bible' in the foundational ethos of Fulcrum when it was founded in 2003; see <www.fulcrum-anglican. org.uk/centre.cfm?menuopt=1>.

177 *Paul: Fresh Perspectives*, p. 18.

178 *Justification*, pp. 26–8; *Anglican Evangelical Identity: Yesterday and Today*, p. 12.

179 *EJG*, p. 77; *Paul: Fresh Perspectives*, pp. 147, 151; *Virtue Reborn*, pp. 57–63, 67–72, 88–92; *Bible, Gospel and Church*, p. 92.

180 *Surprised by Hope*, pp. 205, 296–98.

181 *Virtue Reborn*, pp. 30–8.

182 *Paul: Fresh Perspectives*, p. 147; *Surprised by Hope*, pp. 298–302; *Virtue Reborn*, ch. 6.

183 *Virtue Reborn*, pp. 88–95.

184 *EJG*, pp. 92–5.

185 *Virtue Reborn*, pp. 39–44.

186 *Virtue Reborn*, pp. 44–51.

187 *Virtue Reborn*, pp. 25, 44–51 and particularly ch. 5; *Justification*, pp. 129–30. See also *Following Jesus*, ch. 8.

188 *Virtue Reborn*, p. 81.

189 *EJG*, pp. 62–3; *Surprised by Hope*, pp. 116–17; *Virtue Reborn*, p. 102.

190 *Holy Communion for Amateurs* (London: Hodder/Louisville, KY: Westminster John Knox, 1999), pp. 63–7; *Surprised by Hope*, pp. 284–5; *Simply Christian*, pp. 132–3; *Bible, Gospel and Church*, pp. 107–11; 'Space, Time, Matter and the New Creation', First Address at Calvin College,

Michigan, 6 January 2007, at: <www.calvin.edu/worship/idis/theology/ntwright_sacraments.php>.

191 'Space, Time, Matter and the New Creation'; *Crown and the Fire*, ch. 11.

192 *Holy Communion for Amateurs*, pp. 69–74; *Surprised by Hope*, pp. 286–8; *Simply Christian*, p. 134.

193 *Holy Communion for Amateurs*, pp. 51–5, 73; 'Space, Time, Matter and the New Creation'; *Simply Christian*, pp. 132–3.

194 *Evangelical Anglican Identity*, p. 109.

195 'Sacraments and the New Creation', Second Address at Calvin College, Michigan, 6 January 2007, at: <www.calvin.edu/worship/idis/theology/ntwright_sacraments.php>.

196 'Sacraments and the New Creation'; *Simply Christian*, p. 133.

197 'Sacraments and the New Creation'; *Crown and the Fire*, pp. 65–9.

198 *Paul: Fresh Perspectives*, p. 150; *Surprised by Hope*, pp. 288–92; *Virtue Reborn*, pp. 242–3; *Bible, Gospel and Church*, p. 96; *Simply Christian*, pp. 138–43.

199 *Challenge of Jesus*, p. 146; *EJG*, pp. 76–7; *Surprised by Hope*, p. 292; *Virtue Reborn*, p. 82; *Crown and the Fire*, ch. 10.

200 *JVG*, pp. 292–4; *The Lord and his Prayer* (London: SPCK/Grand Rapids, MI: Eerdmans, 1996); *Simply Christian*, pp. 136–8.

201 *NTPG*, p. 143; *Scripture and the Authority of God*, ch. 3; *Simply Christian*, pp. 154–7; *Evangelical Anglican Identity*, pp. 103–7.

202 *Scripture and the Authority of God*, chs 4–6; *Surprised by Hope*, pp. 293–6.

203 *Scripture and the Authority of God*, pp. 43–4; *Challenge of Jesus*, ch. 7.

204 *NTPG*, pp. 139–44; *Scripture and the Authority of God*, pp. 89–93; *Paul: Fresh Perspectives*, pp. 170–2; *Simply Christian*, p. 159.

205 *NTPG*, p. 141; *Simply Christian*, pp. 159–60.

4 Tom Wright's theology in a pastoral context

1 *New Heavens, New Earth: The Biblical Picture of Christian Hope*, Grove Biblical Series No. 11 (Cambridge: Grove Books, 1999), p. 1.

2 For an interesting analysis of what the death of Princess Diana in 1997 revealed about contemporary culture and conducting Christian ministry within it see Francis Bridger, *The Diana Phenomenon*, Grove Pastoral Series No. 75 (Cambridge: Grove Books, 1998).

3 *Surprised by Hope* (London: SPCK, 2007/San Francisco: Harper One, 2008), pp. 160–4, 183–7.

4 See *New Heavens, New Earth*, pp. 18–19 and *The Resurrection of the Son of God* (London: SPCK/Minneapolis: Fortress, 2003), pp. 165–70 for Wright's analysis of this passage in the context of the Wisdom of Solomon's presentation of eschatology consistent with that of the Old Testament.

5 *Surprised by Hope*, pp. 173–4; *Virtue Reborn* (London: SPCK/San Francisco: Harper One, 2010), pp. 68, 175.

6 For another very helpful treatment of how to interpret the Millennium and its pastoral significance see Michael Gilbertson, *The Meaning of the Millennium*, Grove Biblical Series No. 5 (Cambridge: Grove Books, 1997). See also *The Myth of the Millennium* (London: SPCK/Louisville, KY: Westminster, 1999).

7 'Shipwreck and Kingdom: Acts and the Anglican Communion', closing address at the 13th meeting of the Anglican Consultative Council, in *Living Communion: The Official Report of the 13th Meeting of the Anglican Consultative Council, Nottingham 2005*, ed. J. M. Rosenthal and S. T. Erdey (New York: Church Publishing Incorporated, 2006), pp. 106–18. Also at: <www.fulcrum-anglican.org.uk/news/2005/20050628wright.cfm?doc= 116>; *Surprised by Hope*, p. 122.

8 *New Heavens, New Earth*, p. 17.

9 *New Heavens, New Earth*, p. 25.

10 For examples of the confusion present in many hymns over Christian eschatology see *New Heavens, New Earth*, p. 22; *Surprised by Hope*, pp. 27–30.

5 Tom Wright's theology in a mission context

1 For the story of this, see Stephen Kuhrt, *Church Growth Through the Full Welcome of Children: The Sssh Free Church*, Grove Evangelism Series No. 87 (Cambridge: Grove Books, 2009).

2 For Wright's explanation of the significance of the way that 1 Corinthians 15 ends see *Surprised by Hope* (London: SPCK, 2007/San Francisco: Harper One, 2008), pp. 37, 168–9, 174, 204–5, 219; *Paul for Everyone: 1 Corinthians* (London: SPCK/Louisville, KY: Westminster John Knox, 2003), pp. 224–8.

3 See *Paul for Everyone: 1 Corinthians*, pp. 35–40.

4 *Surprised by Hope*, pp. 220–1.

5 See *Paul for Everyone: 1 Corinthians*, pp. 175–9.

6 *Surprised by Hope*, pp. 244, 279–80; *Virtue Reborn* (London: SPCK/San Francisco: Harper One, 2010), pp. 194–203, particularly 199.

7 Graham Tomlin, *The Provocative Church* (London: SPCK, 2002), particularly pp. 71–86.

8 See Kuhrt, *Sssh Free Church*.

9 *Simply Christian* (London: SPCK/San Francisco: Harper San Francisco, 2006), pp. 3–14.

10 For modern day examples that Wright gives of this see *New Tasks for a Renewed Church* (London: Hodder/Bloomington, MN: Bethany House, 1992), chs 11–13.

11 *What St Paul Really Said* (Oxford: Lion/Grand Rapids, MI: Eerdmans, 1997), ch. 5; *Paul: Fresh Perspectives* (London: SPCK/Minneapolis: Fortress, 2005), p. 163; *Paul for Everyone: Galatians and Thessalonians* (London: SPCK/Louisville, KY: Westminster John Knox, 2002), pp. 87–93.

6 Tom Wright's theology in church life

1 See pages 39–41.

2 Stephen Kuhrt, *Church Growth Through the Full Welcome of Children: The Sssh Free Church*, Grove Evangelism Series No. 87 (Cambridge: Grove Books, 2009).

3 See Kuhrt, *Sssh Free Church*, ch. 3.

4 See Kuhrt, *Sssh Free Church*, p. 18.

5 Wright describes justification by faith as 'the ecumenical doctrine' in *What St Paul Really Said* (Oxford: Lion/Grand Rapids, MI: Eerdmans, 1997), pp. 158–9 and *For All God's Worth* (London: SPCK/Grand Rapids, MI: Eerdmans, 1997), ch. 12.

6 See *Justification: God's Plan and Paul's Vision* (London: SPCK/Downers Grove, IL: Inter-Varsity Press, 2009), pp. 149–50.

7 *What St Paul Really Said*, ch. 7; *Paul: Fresh Perspectives* (London: SPCK/Minneapolis: Fortress, 2005), pp. 158–9; *Justification*, p. 94.

8 By far the most helpful of Wright's books here has been the relatively less well known *New Tasks for a Renewed Church* (London: Hodder/Bloomington, MN: Bethany House, 1992), which has lots of detail on idolatry and dualism and examples of both in the ancient and modern world. See also *Following Jesus: Biblical Reflections on Christian Discipleship* (London: SPCK/Grand Rapids, MI: Eerdmans, 1994), ch. 9.

9 *New Tasks*, pp. 27–39.

10 *New Tasks*, pp. 32–4; *Simply Christian* (London: SPCK/San Francisco: Harper San Francisco, 2006), p. 127.

11 *New Tasks*, pp. 28–9.

12 *Surprised by Hope* (London: SPCK, 2007/San Francisco: Harper One, 2008), pp. 233–6; *Simply Christian*, pp. 200–2; *Virtue Reborn* (London: SPCK/San Francisco: Harper One, 2010), pp. 71–2, 200.

13 Wright's emphasis upon the practical importance of the doctrine of the Trinity in combating idolatry and dualism is found in *New Tasks*, chs 15–16.

14 *Simply Christian*, ch. 2.

15 Kuhrt, *Sssh Free Church*, pp. 6–8.

16 Kuhrt, *Sssh Free Church*, pp. 11–19.

17 See pages 59–61.

18 For a helpful treatment of this theme see also Graham Tomlin, *Spiritual Fitness: Christian Character in a Consumer Culture* (London, New York: Continuum, 2006).

19 *The Resurrection of the Son of God* (London: SPCK/Minneapolis: Fortress, 2003), ch. 6.

20 An important theme of *Evil and the Justice of God* (London: SPCK/Downers Grove, IL: Inter-Varsity Press, 2006), particularly ch. 5.

21 *Simply Christian*, pp. 130–1.

22 See pages 42 and 60 and *EJG*, ch. 5.

23 *Virtue Reborn*, especially ch. 7.

24 *Anglican Evangelical Identity: Yesterday and Today* (London: Latimer Trust, 2008), p. 18; *Simply Christian*, p. 129; *Scripture and the Authority of God* (London: SPCK/San Francisco: Harper San Francisco, 2005), pp. 95–7; *Virtue Reborn*, p. 192.

25 *Simply Christian*, p. 130; *Virtue Reborn*, pp. 191–2.

26 *For All God's Worth*, chs 2 and 24.

27 *Anglican Evangelical Identity*, pp. 18–19.

28 See Kuhrt, *Sssh Free Church*, pp. 8–10.

29 'Women's Service in the Church: The Biblical Basis', paper for a symposium on 'Men, Women and the Church' at St John's College, Durham, 4 September 2004.

30 *Paul for Everyone: 1 Corinthians* (London: SPCK/Louisville, KY: Westminster John Knox, 2003), pp. 138–43. For Wright's treatment of 1 Timothy 2.8–15 see *Paul for Everyone: The Pastoral Letters* (London: SPCK/Louisville, KY: Westminster John Knox, 2003), pp. 21–7.

31 See particularly David Murrow, *Why Men Hate Coming to Church* (Nashville, TN: Nelson, 2005).

32 For a strong argument against this, see R. T. France, *A Slippery Slope? The Ordination of Women and Homosexual Practice – A Case Study in Biblical Interpretation*, Grove Biblical Series No. 16 (Cambridge: Grove Books, 2000).

33 'Communion and Koinonia: Pauline Reflections on Tolerance and Boundaries', paper given by N. T. Wright to the Future of Anglicanism Conference, Oxford, 2002, at: <www.ntwrightpage.com/Wright_Communion_Koinonia.htm>.

34 See *Surprised by Hope*, pp. 187–96; *Following Jesus*, ch. 10; *For All the Saints*, pp. 42–6.

35 *Paul for Everyone: The Prison Letters* (London: SPCK/Louisville, KY: Westminster John Knox, 2002), pp. 64–8.

36 See chs 14–15 on 'Reshaping the Church for Mission' in *Surprised by Hope* and Part Two of *New Tasks*.

37 Some of Wright's concerns about the agenda of making worship more accessible and informal can be found in *For All God's Worth*, p. 73 and *Simply Christian*, p. 130. In other places, however, Wright does speak of the need for 'translating the message and challenge of Jesus into categories appropriate for a different culture and place'; see *For All God's Worth*, p. 132.

7 The challenge of Tom Wright to the Church

1 *Justification: God's Plan and Paul's Vision* (London: SPCK/Downers Grove, IL: Inter-Varsity Press, 2009), pp. 20–1.

2 For significant attempts to persuade the evangelical tradition to persevere with this approach see the addresses from the Evangelical Anglican leaders conference held in January 1995, published in Gordon Kuhrt (ed.), *To Proclaim Afresh: Evangelical Agenda for the Church* (London: SPCK, 1995). See also R. T. France and A. E. McGrath, *Evangelical Anglicans: Their Role and Influence in the Church Today* (London: SPCK, 1993), and Alister McGrath, *Evangelicalism and the Future of Christianity* (London: Hodder and Stoughton, 1994).

3 John Stott with David Edwards, *Essentials: A Liberal-Evangelical Dialogue* (Sevenoaks: Hodder and Stoughton, 1988), p. 88.

4 See particularly Melvin Tinker (ed.), *The Anglican Evangelical Crisis: A Radical Agenda for a Bible Based Church* (Fearn: Christian Focus, 1995). For an interesting debate on from both perspectives on this see Charles Yeats (ed.), *Has Keele Failed?: Reform in the Church of England* (London: Hodder and Stoughton, 1995), particularly pp. 43–80.

5 See Dave Tomlinson, *The Post Evangelical* (London: Triangle, 1995); Steve Chalke and Alan Mann, *The Lost Message of Jesus* (Grand Rapids, MI: Zondervan, 2003).

6 See <www.fulcrum-anglican.org.uk>.

7 See <http://.covenant-communion.net>.

8 'God's Richly Varied Wisdom: A sermon preached at the national launch of Fulcrum', Holy Trinity Church, Clapham, 5 November 2003, at: <www.fulfrum-anglican.org.uk/?118>.

9 See also Wright's later reflections upon the GAFCON movement and the so-called 'Covenant for the Church of England': 'After GAFCON: Reflections by the Bishop of Durham', June 2008, at: <www.fulcrum-anglican.org.uk/?317>; 'Further thoughts on GAFCON and related matters', July 2008, at: <www.fulcrum-anglican.org.uk/?324>; and 'A Confused Covenant: Initial comments on "A Covenant for the Church of England"', issued by Paul Perkin and Chris Sugden and others', at: <www.fulcrum-anglican.org.uk/news/2006/20061214wright.cfm?doc=171>.

10 'God's Richly Varied Wisdom'.

11 See the works of John Stott, particularly *Christ the Controversialist: The Basics of Belief* (Leicester: Inter-Varsity Press, 1970); *The Authentic Jesus: A Response to Current Scepticism in the Church* (Basingstoke: Marshall Pickering, 1985); and with David Edwards, *Essentials.*

12 For Wright's response to postmodern approaches to Scripture see *The New Testament and the People of God* (London: SPCK/Minneapolis: Fortress, 1992), Parts I and II; and *Scripture and the Authority of God* (London: SPCK/San Francisco: Harper San Francisco, 2005), p. 82.

13 The ideas in this paragraph were first sketched out in my article 'Discovering a Positive Model for Responding to Unorthodox Theology', again written with an autobiographical perspective <www.fulcrum-anglican.org.uk/news/2006/20060208kuhrt.cfm?doc=85>.

14 The title Oliver O'Donovan later gave to a series of articles first published on the Fulcrum website under the title 'Sermons on the Subject of the Day' and later republished in *A Conversation Waiting to Begin: The Churches and the Gay Controversy* (London: SCM Press, 2009).

Bibliography

Works by N. T. Wright (sometimes as 'Tom Wright')
Books (in date order)

Virtue Reborn (US title: *After You Believe*). London: SPCK/San Francisco: Harper One (2010).

Lent for Everyone: Luke. London: SPCK (2009).

For Everyone Bible Study Guides. Based on the *For Everyone* commentaries, adapted by editors at IVP. Downers Grove, IL: Inter-Varsity Press/London: SPCK. Volumes so far: *Matthew, Mark, Romans, 1 Corinthians, Ephesians, Colossians and Philemon, 1 and 2 Thessalonians, 1 and 2 Timothy* and *Titus*. Others are in preparation.

Justification: God's Plan and Paul's Vision. London: SPCK/Downers Grove, IL: Inter-Varsity Press (2009).

Anglican Evangelical Identity: Yesterday and Today (with J. I. Packer). Reissue of booklet published in 1980, with substantial new preface. London: Latimer Trust (2008).

Theological Interpretation of the New Testament: A Book-by-Book Survey, K. J. Vanhoozer (gen. ed.), D. J. Treier and N. T. Wright (assoc. eds) (volume consisting of the specifically New Testament material extracted from *Dictionary for Theological Interpretation of Scripture*). Grand Rapids, MI/ London: SPCK (2008).

Jesus: The Final Days (with Craig A. Evans), ed. Troy A. Miller. London: SPCK/ Louisville, KY: Westminster John Knox (2008). Chapter 3 is by NTW, overlapping substantially with Chapters 3 and 4 of *Surprised by Hope*.

Acts for Everyone. London: SPCK/Louisville, KY: Westminster John Knox (2008).

Surprised by Hope. London: SPCK (2007). US edition San Francisco: Harper One (2008) with subtitle *Rethinking Heaven, Resurrection and the Mission of the Church*.

The Cross and the Colliery (US title: *Christians at the Cross*). London: SPCK/ Ijamsville, MD: The Word Among Us Press (2007).

Judas and the Gospel of Jesus. London: SPCK/Grand Rapids, MI: Baker Books (2006).

Evil and the Justice of God. London: SPCK/Downers Grove, IL: Inter-Varsity Press (2006).

Decoding Da Vinci: The Challenge of Historic Christianity to Conspiracy and Fantasy, Grove Biblical Series B39. Cambridge: Grove Books (2006).

Simply Christian. London: SPCK/San Francisco: Harper San Francisco (2006).

The Resurrection of Jesus: John Dominic Crossan and N. T. Wright in Dialogue, ed. Robert B. Stewart. Minneapolis: Fortress (2006).

The Scriptures, the Cross, and the Power of God. London: SPCK/Louisville, KY: Westminster John Knox (2005).

Paul: Fresh Perspectives (US title: *Paul in Fresh Perspective*). London: SPCK/ Minneapolis: Fortress (2005).

Scripture and the Authority of God (US title: *The Last Word: Beyond the Bible Wars to a New Understanding of the Authority of Scripture*). London: SPCK/ San Francisco: Harper San Francisco (2005).

Dictionary for Theological Interpretation of Scripture, ed. with K. Vanhoozer et al. Grand Rapids, MI: Baker Books/London: SPCK (2005).

Paul for Everyone: Romans (two vols). London: SPCK/Louisville, KY: Westminster John Knox (2004).

For All the Saints? Remembering the Christian Departed. London: SPCK/ Harrisburg, PA: Morehouse (2003).

Hebrews for Everyone. London: SPCK/Louisville, KY: Westminster John Knox (2003).

Paul for Everyone: The Pastoral Letters. London: SPCK/Louisville, KY: Westminster John Knox (2003).

Quiet Moments (selected highlights from *A Moment of . . .* series, 1997). Oxford: Lion (2003).

The Resurrection of the Son of God (*Christian Origins and the Question of God*, Vol. 3). London: SPCK/Minneapolis: Fortress (2003).

Paul for Everyone: 1 Corinthians. London: SPCK/Louisville, KY: Westminster John Knox (2003).

Paul for Everyone: 2 Corinthians. London: SPCK/Louisville, KY: Westminster John Knox (2003).

John for Everyone (two vols). London: SPCK/Louisville, KY: Westminster John Knox (2002).

Paul for Everyone: The Prison Letters. London: SPCK/Louisville, KY: Westminster John Knox (2002).

The Contemporary Quest for Jesus (edited extracts from *Jesus and the Victory of God*, chs 1–3). Minneapolis: Fortress (2002).

The Meal Jesus Gave Us (reissue of *Holy Communion for Amateurs*). London: Hodder/Louisville, KY: Westminster John Knox (2002).

Romans, in *The New Interpreter's Bible*. Vol. X, 393–770. Nashville, TN: Abingdon (2002).

Twelve Months of Sundays: Reflections on Bible Readings, Year B. London: SPCK (2002).

Matthew for Everyone (two vols). London: SPCK/Louisville, KY: Westminster John Knox (2002).

Paul for Everyone: Galatians and Thessalonians. London: SPCK/Louisville, KY: Westminster John Knox (2002).

Luke for Everyone. London: SPCK/Louisville, KY: Westminster John Knox (2001).

Mark for Everyone. London: SPCK/Louisville, KY: Westminster John Knox (2001).

Twelve Months of Sundays: Reflections on Bible Readings, Year A. London: SPCK (2001).

Twelve Months of Sundays: Reflections on Bible Readings, Year C. London: SPCK (2000).

Holy Communion for Amateurs. London: Hodder/Louisville, KY: Westminster John Knox (1999) (reissued in 2002 as *The Meal Jesus Gave Us*).

The Challenge of Jesus. Downers Grove, IL: Inter-Varsity Press/London: SPCK (1999).

Romans and the People of God: Essays in Honor of Gordon D. Fee on the Occasion of his 65th Birthday (ed. with Sven K. Soderlund). Grand Rapids, MI: Eerdmans (1999).

New Heavens, New Earth: The Biblical Picture of Christian Hope, Grove Biblical Series No. 11. Cambridge: Grove Books (1999).

The Millennium Myth (UK title: *The Myth of the Millennium*). London: SPCK/Louisville, KY: Westminster (1999).

The Way of the Lord: Christian Pilgrimage in the Holy Land and Beyond. London: SPCK/Grand Rapids, MI: Eerdmans (1999).

The Meaning of Jesus: Two Visions (with Marcus J. Borg). San Francisco: Harper San Francisco/London: SPCK (1999).

Reflecting the Glory. Oxford: Bible Reading Fellowship/Minneapolis: Augsburg (1997).

A Moment of Prayer; A Moment of Quiet; A Moment of Peace; A Moment of Celebration (four separate small volumes). Oxford: Lion/Grand Rapids, MI: Eerdmans (1997).

What St Paul Really Said. Oxford: Lion/Grand Rapids, MI: Eerdmans (1997).

For All God's Worth. London: SPCK/Grand Rapids, MI: Eerdmans (1997).

Jesus and the Victory of God (*Christian Origins and the Question of God*, Vol. 2). London: SPCK/Minneapolis: Fortress (1996).

The Original Jesus. Oxford: Lion/Grand Rapids, MI: Eerdmans (1996).

The Lord and his Prayer. London: SPCK/Grand Rapids, MI: Eerdmans (1996).

Following Jesus: Biblical Reflections on Christian Discipleship. London: SPCK/Grand Rapids, MI: Eerdmans (1994).

Who Was Jesus? London: SPCK/Grand Rapids, MI: Eerdmans (1992).

The New Testament and the People of God (*Christian Origins and the Question of God*, Vol. 1). London: SPCK/Minneapolis: Fortress (1992).

The Crown and the Fire. London: SPCK/Grand Rapids, MI: Eerdmans (1992).

New Tasks for a Renewed Church (US title: *Bringing the Church to the World*). London: Hodder/Bloomington, MN: Bethany House (1992).

The Climax of the Covenant: Christ and the Law in Pauline Theology. Edinburgh: T & T Clark (1991)/Minneapolis: Fortress (1992).

The Interpretation of the New Testament, 1861–1986 (with Stephen Neill). Oxford: Oxford University Press (1988).

The Glory of Christ in the New Testament: Studies in Christology in Memory of George Bradford Caird (ed. with L. D. Hurst). Oxford: Oxford University Press (1987).

The Epistles of Paul to the Colossians and to Philemon. Leicester: Tyndale/Grand Rapids, MI: Eerdmans (1986).

The Work of John Frith, Courtenay Library of Reformation Classics No. 7. Appleford: Sutton Courtenay Press (1983).

Small Faith, Great God: Biblical Faith for Today's Christians. Eastbourne: Kingsway/New Jersey: Revell (1978).

The Grace of God in the Gospel (with John Cheeseman, Philip Gardner and Michael Sadgrove). Edinburgh: Banner of Truth (1972).

Major articles (in date order)

'Romans 9—11 and the "New Perspective"', in *Between Gospel and Election: Explorations in the Interpretation of Romans 9—11*, ed. Florian Wilk and J. Ross Wagner, with Frank Schleritt. WUNT. Tübingen: Mohr, pp. 37–54 (2010).

'A Scripture-Formed Communion? Possibilities and Prospects after Lambeth, ACC and General Convention', *Journal of Anglican Studies*, Vol. 7.2, pp. 1–19 (2009).

'Reading Paul, Thinking Scripture', in *Scripture's Doctrine and Theology's Bible: How the New Testament Shapes Christian Dogmatics*, ed. Markus Bockmuehl and Alan J. Torrance. Grand Rapids, MI: Baker Academic, pp. 59–71 (2008).

'Faith, Virtue, Justification and the Journey to Freedom', in *The Word Leaps the Gap: Essays on Scripture and Theology Sparked in Honor of Richard B. Hays*, ed. J. R. Wagner, C. K. Rowe and A. K. Grieb. Grand Rapids, MI: Eerdmans, pp. 472–97 (2008).

'Kingdom Come: The Public Meaning of the Gospels', *The Christian Century*, 17 June, pp. 29–34 (2008).

'God in Public? Reflections on Faith and Society', *Justice Journal*, 5(1), pp. 17–36 (with a comment by Rabinder Singh QC) (2008).

'Christian Origins and the Question of God', in *Engaging the Doctrine of God: Contemporary Protestant Perspectives*, ed. Bruce L. McCormack. Grand Rapids, MI: Baker Academic/Edinburgh: Rutherford House, pp. 21–36 (2008).

'Paul as Preacher: The Gospel Then and Now', *Irish Theological Quarterly*, 72, pp. 131–46 (2007).

'The Reasons for Jesus' Crucifixion', in *Stricken by God? Nonviolent Identification and the Victory of Christ*, ed. B. Jersack and M. Hardin (reprint of ch. 12 of *Jesus and the Victory of God*). Abbotsford, Canada: Fresh Wind Press, pp. 78–149 (2007).

'4QMMT and Paul: Justification, "Works," and Eschatology', in *History and Exegesis: New Testament Essays in Honor of Dr E. Earle Ellis for His 80th Birthday*, ed. Sang-Won (Aaron) Son. New York and London: T & T Clark, pp. 104–32 (2006).

'New Perspectives on Paul', in *Justification in Perspective: Historical Developments and Contemporary Challenges*, ed. Bruce L. McCormack. Grand Rapids, MI: Baker Academic, pp. 243–64 (2006).

'Shipwreck and Kingdom: Acts and the Anglican Communion', closing address at the 13th meeting of the Anglican Consultative Council, in *Living Communion: The Official Report of the 13th Meeting of the Anglican Consultative Council, Nottingham 2005*, ed. J. M. Rosenthal and S. T. Erdey. New York: Church Publishing Incorporated, pp. 106–18 (2006).

'Witness and Wisdom' (on Robert Browning and the tasks facing a modern Christian university), *Studies in Browning and His Circle* (Baylor University), 26(2), September, pp. 124–34 (2005).

'Doubts about Doubt: *Honest to God* Forty Years On', *Journal of Anglican Studies*, 3(2), pp. 181–96 (2005).

'Resurrecting Old Arguments: Responding to Four Essays', *Journal for the Study of the Historical Jesus*, 3(2), pp. 187–209 (2005).

'God and Caesar, Then and Now', in *The Character of Wisdom: Essays in Honour of Wesley Carr*, ed. Martyn Percy and Stephen Lowe. London: Ashgate, pp. 157–71 (2004).

'Redemption from the New Perspective', in *Redemption*, ed. S. T. Davis, D. Kendall and G. O'Collins. Oxford: Oxford University Press, pp. 69–100 (2004).

'Women's Service in the Church: The Biblical Basis', paper for a symposium on 'Men, Women and the Church' at St John's College, Durham, 4 September 2004.

'Freedom and Framework, Spirit and Truth: Recovering Biblical Worship', *Studia Liturgica* 32, pp. 176–95 (2002).

'Jesus' Self-Understanding', in *The Incarnation*, ed. S. T. Davis, D. Kendall and G. O'Collins. Oxford: Oxford University Press, pp. 47–61 (2002).

'Jesus' Resurrection and Christian Origins', *Gregorianum*, 83(4), pp. 615–35. Abridged and adapted in *Passionate Conviction: Contemporary Discourses on Christian Apologetics*, ed. Paul Copan and William Lane Craig. Nashville, TN: B & H Publishing Group, pp. 123–37 (2002).

'Communion and Koinonia: Pauline Reflections on Tolerance and Boundaries', paper given at the Future of Anglicanism Conference, Oxford, 2002. <www.ntwrightpage.com/Wright_Communion_Koinonia. htm>.

'Resurrection: From Theology to Music and Back Again', in *Sounding the Depths: Theology Through the Arts*, ed. J. Begbie. London: SCM Press, pp. 193–202 (2002).

'Paul and Caesar: A New Reading of Romans', in *A Royal Priesthood: The Use of the Bible Ethically and Politically*, ed. C. Bartholemew. Carlisle: Paternoster Press, pp. 173–93 (2002). A lightly rewritten version of 'A Fresh Perspective on Paul?'

'Coming Home to St Paul? Reading Romans a Hundred Years after Charles Gore', *Scottish Journal of Theology*, 55, pp. 392–407 (2002).

'A Fresh Perspective on Paul?', *Bulletin of the John Rylands Library*, 83(1), pp. 21–39 (2001).

'The Lord's Prayer as a Paradigm of Christian Prayer', in *Into God's Presence: Prayer in the New Testament*, ed. R. L. Longenecker. Grand Rapids, MI: Eerdmans, pp. 132–54 (2001).

'Jesus and the Resurrection', in *Jesus Then and Now: Images of Jesus in History and Christology*, ed. Marvin Meyer and Charles Hughes. Harrisburg, PA: Trinity Press International, pp. 54–71 (2001).

'New Heavens, New Earth', in *Called to One Hope: Perspectives on Life to Come. Drew Lectures on Immortality Delivered at Spurgeon's College,* ed. John Colwell. Carlisle: Paternoster Press, pp. 31–51 (2000).

'Paul's Gospel and Caesar's Empire', in *Paul and Politics: Ekklesia, Israel, Imperium, Interpretation. Essays in Honor of Krister Stendahl,* ed. Richard A. Horsley. Harrisburg, PA: Trinity Press International, pp. 160–83 (2000).

'Resurrection in Q?', in *Christology, Controversy and Community: New Testament Essays in Honour of David R. Catchpole,* ed. D. G. Horrell and C. M. Tuckett. Leiden: Brill, pp. 85–97 (2000).

'Gospels', in *Oxford Companion to Christian Thought,* ed. A. Hastings. Oxford: Oxford University Press, pp. 274–6 (2000).

'The Letter to the Galatians: Exegesis and Theology', in *Between Two Horizons: Spanning New Testament Studies and Systematic Theology,* ed. Joel B. Green and Max Turner. Grand Rapids, MI: Eerdmans, pp. 205–36 (2000).

'A New Birth?' (review article of J. D. Crossan's *The Birth of Christianity*), *Scottish Journal of Theology,* 53(1), pp. 72–91 (2000).

'In Grateful Dialogue: A Response', in *Jesus and the Restoration of Israel: A Critical Assessment of N. T. Wright's Jesus and the Victory of God,* ed. Carey Newman. Downer's Grove, IL: Inter-Varsity Press, pp. 234–68, 306–9 (1999).

'Paul's Gospel and Caesar's Empire', *Center of Theological Inquiry Reflections* (Princeton), 2, pp. 42–65 (1999).

'The Biblical Formation of a Doctrine of Christ', in *Who Do You Say that I Am? Christology and the Church,* ed. Donald Armstrong. Grand Rapids, MI: Eerdmans, pp. 47–68 (1999).

'New Exodus, New Inheritance: The Narrative Substructure of Romans 3—8', in *Romans and the People of God: Essays in Honor of Gordon D. Fee on the Occasion of his 65th Birthday,* ed. S. K. Soderlund and N. T. Wright. Grand Rapids, MI: Eerdmans, pp. 26–35 (1999).

'Five Gospels but No Gospel: Jesus and the Seminar', in *Authenticating the Activities of Jesus,* ed. Bruce Chilton and Craig A. Evans. Leiden: Brill, pp. 83–120 (1999).

'Theology, History and Jesus: A Response to Maurice Casey and Clive Marsh', *Journal for the Study of the New Testament,* 69, pp. 105–12 (1998).

'Jesus and the Quest', in *The Truth About Jesus,* ed. Donald Armstrong. Grand Rapids, MI: Eerdmans, pp. 4–25 (1998).

'Christian Origins and the Resurrection of Jesus: (1) The Resurrection of Jesus as a Historical Problem', *Sewannee Theological Review,* 41(2), pp. 107–23; '(2) Early Traditions and the Origins of Christianity', pp. 125–40; '(3) The Resurrection and the Postmodern Dilemma', pp. 141–56 (1998).

'Jesus and the Identity of God', *Ex Auditu*, 14, pp. 42–56 (1998).

'The Servant and Jesus: The Relevance of the Colloquy for the Current Quest for Jesus', in *Jesus and the Suffering Servant: Isaiah 53 and Christian Origins*, ed. William H. Bellinger, Jr and William R. Farmer. Harrisburg, PA: Trinity Press International, pp. 281–97 (1998).

'Doing Justice to Jesus: A Response to J. D. Crossan, "What Victory? What God?"', *Scottish Journal of Theology*, 50(3), pp. 359–79 (1997).

'A Biblical Portrait of God', in *The Changing Face of God: Lincoln Lectures in Theology 1996*, Lincoln Studies in Theology 2, ed. N. T. Wright, Keith Ward and Brian Hebblethwaite. Lincoln: Lincoln Cathedral Publications, pp. 9–29 (1996).

'Jesus', in *Early Christian Thought in its Jewish Context*, ed. John Barclay and John Sweet. Cambridge: Cambridge University Press, 43–58 (1996).

'Paul, Arabia and Elijah (Galatians 1:17)', *Journal of Biblical Literature*, 115, pp. 683–92 (1996).

'The Law in Romans 2', in *Paul and the Mosaic Law*, ed. J. D. G. Dunn. Tübingen: Mohr, pp. 131–50 (1996).

'Romans and the Theology of Paul', in *Pauline Theology, Vol. III*, ed. David M. Hay and E. Elizabeth Johnson. Minneapolis: Fortress, pp. 30–67 (republished with minor alterations from *SBL 1992 Seminar Papers*, ed. E. H. Lovering, pp. 184–213) (1995).

'Two Radical Jews: A Review Article of Daniel Boyarin, *A Radical Jew: Paul and the Politics of Identity*', *Reviews in Religion and Theology*, 3 (August), pp. 15–23 (1995).

'Gospel and Theology in Galatians', in *Gospel in Paul: Studies on Corinthians, Galatians and Romans for Richard N. Longenecker*, ed. L. Ann Jervis and Peter Richardson, pp. 222–239. *Journal for the Study of the New Testament*, Supplement Series 108. Sheffield: Sheffield Academic Press (1994).

'On Becoming the Righteousness of God: 2 Corinthians 5:21', in *Pauline Theology, Vol. II*, ed. D. M. Hay. Minneapolis: Augsburg Fortress, pp. 200–8 (1993).

'Taking the Text with her Pleasure: A Post-Post-Modernist Response to J. Dominic Crossan, *The Historical Jesus: The Life of a Mediterranean Jewish Peasant* (with apologies to A. A. Milne, St Paul, and James Joyce)', *Theology*, 96, pp. 303–10 (1993).

'Romans and Pauline Theology', in *SBL 1992 Seminar Papers*, ed. E. H. Lovering. Atlanta, GA: Scholars Press (1992).

'Quest for the Historical Jesus', in *Anchor Bible Dictionary*, ed. D. N. Freedman, vol. 3. New York: Doubleday, pp. 796–802 (1992).

'One God, One Lord, One People: Incarnational Christology for a Church in a Pagan Environment', *Ex Auditu*, 7, pp. 45–58 (1991).

'How can the Bible be Authoritative?', *Vox Evangelica*, 21, pp. 7–32 (1991).

'Putting Paul Together Again', in *Pauline Theology, Vol. 1: Thessalonians, Philippians, Galatians, Philemon*, ed. J. Bassler. Minneapolis: Augsburg Fortress, pp. 183–211 (1991). Adapted and reprinted in *The Climax of the Covenant: Christ and the Law in Pauline Theology*, ch. 1.

'Poetry and Theology in Colossians 1:15–20', *New Testament Studies*, 30, pp. 444–68 (1990). Reprinted in *The Climax of the Covenant*, ch. 5.

'Reflected Glory? 2 Corinthians iii.18', in *The Glory of Christ in the New Testament: Studies in Christology in Memory of George Bradford Caird*, ed. N. T. Wright and L. D. Hurst. Oxford: Oxford University Press, pp. 139–50 (1987).

'"Constraints" and the Jesus of History', *Scottish Journal of Theology*, 9(2), pp. 189–210 (1986).

':ρπαγμος and the Meaning of Philippians 2.5–11', *Journal of Theological Studies*, 37(2), pp. 321–52 (1986).

'Jesus, Israel and the Cross', in *SBL 1985 Seminar Papers*, ed. K. H. Richards. Chico, CA: Scholars Press, pp. 75–95 (1985).

'Adam in Pauline Christology', in *SBL 1983 Seminar Papers*, ed. K. H. Richards. Chico, CA: Scholars Press, pp. 359–89 (1983).

'A New Tübingen School? Ernst Käsemann and his Significance', *Themelios*, 7, pp. 6–16 (1982).

'Where Shall Doctrine Be Found?' in *Believing in the Church: The Corporate Nature of Faith*, Report by the Doctrine Commission of the Church of England. London: SPCK, pp. 108–41 (1981).

Evangelical Anglican Identity: The Connection Between Bible, Gospel and Church, Latimer Studies No. 8. Oxford: Latimer (1980). Republished in *Anglican Evangelical Identity: Yesterday and Today* (2008).

'The Meaning of περι :μαρτιας in Romans 8:3', in *Studia Biblica 1978*, vol. 3, ed. E. A. Livingstone. Sheffield: JSOT Press, pp. 453–9 (1980).

'The Paul of History and the Apostle of Faith', *Tyndale Bulletin*, 29, pp. 61–88 (1978).

'Jesus Christ the Only Saviour' (with M. Sadgrove) in *Obeying Christ in a Changing World, Vol. 1: The Lord Christ*, ed. J. R. W. Stott. London: Collins, pp. 161–89 (1977).

Other books referred to

Ken Bailey, *Jacob and the Prodigal: How Jesus Retold Israel's Story*, Oxford: Bible Reading Fellowship/Downers Grove, IL: Inter-Varsity Press (2003).

Francis Bridger, *The Diana Phenomenon*, Grove Pastoral Series No. 75. Cambridge: Grove Books (1998).

Steve Chalke and Alan Mann, *The Lost Message of Jesus*. Grand Rapids, MI: Zondervan (2003).

Stephen Cottrell, *Sacrament, Wholeness and Evangelism: A Catholic Approach*, Grove Evangelism Series No. 33. Cambridge: Grove Books (1996).

Graham Cray et al., *The Post Evangelical Debate*. London: Triangle (1997).

P. Crowe, *Keele '67 – the National Evangelical Anglican Congress Statement*. London: Falcon Books (1967).

J. D. Douglas (ed.), *Let the Earth Hear His Voice: International Congress on World Evangelisation, Lausanne, Switzerland*. Minneapolis: World Wide Publications (1975).

Timothy Dudley-Smith, *John Stott: A Global Ministry*. Leicester: Inter-Varsity Press (2001).

R. T. France and A. E. McGrath, *Evangelical Anglicans: Their Role and Influence in the Church Today*. London: SPCK (1993).

R. T. France, *A Slippery Slope? The Ordination of Women and Homosexual Practice – A Case Study in Biblical Interpretation*, Grove Biblical Series No. 16. Cambridge: Grove Books (2000).

Paul Gardner, Chris Wright and Chris Green (eds), *Fanning the Flame: Bible, Cross and Mission: Meeting the Challenge in a Changing World*. Grand Rapids, MI: Zondervan (2003).

Michael Gilbertson, *The Meaning of the Millennium*, Grove Biblical Series No. 5. Cambridge: Grove Books (1997).

Steve Jeffrey, Mike Ovey and Andrew Sach, *Pierced for Our Transgressions: Rediscovering the Glory of Penal Substitution*. Nottingham: Inter-Varsity Press (2007).

Gordon Kuhrt (ed.), *Doctrine Matters*. London: Hodder (1993).

Gordon Kuhrt (ed.), *To Proclaim Afresh: Evangelical Agenda for the Church*. London: SPCK (1995).

Stephen Kuhrt, *Church Growth Through the Full Welcome of Children: The Sssh Free Church*, Grove Evangelism Series No. 87. Cambridge: Grove Books (2009).

Alister McGrath, *Evangelicalism and the Future of Christianity*. London: Hodder and Stoughton (1994).

David Murrow, *Why Men Hate Coming to Church*. Nashville, TN: Nelson (2005).

Connie Neal, *The Gospel According to Harry Potter*. Louisville, KY: John Knox Press (2002).

H. Richard Niebuhr, *Christ and Culture*. New York: Harper Collins (1951).

Oliver O'Donovan, *A Conversation Waiting to Begin: The Churches and the Gay Controversy*. London: SCM Press (2009).

John Piper, *The Future of Justification: A Response to N. T. Wright*. Nottingham: Inter-Varsity Press (2008).

E. P. Sanders, *Paul and Palestinian Judaism: A Comparison of Patterns of Religion*. London: SCM Press/Philadelphia: Fortress (1977).

E. P. Sanders, *Paul, the Law and the Jewish People*. Philadelphia: Fortress/London: SCM Press (1983).

E. P. Sanders, *Paul*, Past Masters. Oxford: Oxford University Press (1991).

Christopher Sandford, *McQueen: The Biography*. London: Harper Collins (2001).

Ronald J. Sider, with a Response by John R. W. Stott, *Evangelism, Salvation and Social Justice*, Grove Ethics Series No. 16. Bramcote: Grove Books (1977).

M. Stibbe and J. John, *Passion for the Movies*. Milton Keynes: Authentic (2005).

J. R. W. Stott, *Christ the Controversialist: The Basics of Belief*. Leicester: Inter-Varsity Press (1970).

J. R. W. Stott, *The Authentic Jesus: A Response to Current Scepticism in the Church*. Basingstoke: Marshall Pickering (1985).

J. R. W. Stott, *'What is the Spirit saying . . .': A Report on NEAC3*. London: Church of England Evangelical Council (1988).

J. R. W. Stott with David Edwards, *Essentials: A Liberal-Evangelical Dialogue*. Sevenoaks: Hodder and Stoughton (1988).

J. R. W. Stott, *New Issues Facing Christians Today*. London: Collins/Marshall Pickering (1999).

Michael B. Thompson, *The New Perspective on Paul*, Grove Biblical Series No. 26. Cambridge: Grove Books (2002).

Melvin Tinker (ed.), *The Anglican Evangelical Crisis: A Radical Agenda for a Bible Based Church*. Fearn: Christian Focus (1995).

Graham Tomlin, *The Provocative Church*. London: SPCK (2002).

Graham Tomlin, *Spiritual Fitness: Christian Character in a Consumer Culture*. London, New York: Continuum (2006).

Dave Tomlinson, *The Post Evangelical*. London: Triangle (1995).

C. M. Tuckett, *Christology and the New Testament: Jesus and his Earliest Followers*. Edinburgh: Edinburgh University Press (2001).

Charles Yeats (ed.), *Has Keele Failed?: Reform in the Church of England*. London: Hodder and Stoughton (1995).

Index of names

Index of topics

Index of topics